Cyberviolence against Women

This title explores the growing phenomenon of cyberviolence against women, analyzing its causes, manifestations, and consequences from a multidisciplinary perspective.

It aims to fill the gap in existing literature by not only diagnosing the issue but also providing comprehensive legal and policy solutions. Unlike other works, this book uniquely integrates perspectives from human rights law, digital governance, gender studies, and cybersecurity, making it both an academic resource and a practical guide for policymakers and advocates. Cyberviolence against women is a pressing global issue, merging the long-recognized problem of gender-based violence with the pervasive reach of digital technology.

With insights from legal frameworks and expert recommendations, it is an essential resource for policymakers, academics, and advocates committed to tackling online gender-based violence.

Sylwia Spurek is a former Member of the European Parliament (2019–2024) and Deputy Human Rights Commissioner of Poland (2015–2019), attorney-at-law and legislator, law and public policy expert in the field of equal treatment and counteracting violence against women and gender-based violence (domestic violence and cyberviolence against women in particular).

Routledge Frontiers of Criminal Justice

Legal Implications of Taser Use and Prone Position on Excited Delirium Subjects
Vidisha Barua Worley

Through the Distorted Lens
Constructing Truth and Reality with Legal Narratives
Fiona C. Hum

Youth Diversion
Exploring Criminal Justice Perspectives through An Australian Case Study
Estrella Pearce

Beyond Autoethnography
Lived Experience Criminology
Dwayne Antojado, Danica Darley, and Matthew Maycock

The Psychology of Eyewitness Identification
Exploring the Relationship Between Traditional and Alternative Approaches to Recognition
Dominic T. Jordan, Adrian J. Scott, and Donald M. Thomson

Cyberviolence against Women
A New Face of an Old Problem
Sylwia Spurek

For more information about this series, please visit: www.routledge.com/Routledge-Frontiers-of-Criminal-Justice/book-series/RFCJ

Cyberviolence against Women

A New Face of an Old Problem

Sylwia Spurek

Routledge
Taylor & Francis Group
NEW YORK AND LONDON

First published 2026
by Routledge
605 Third Avenue, New York, NY 10158

and by Routledge
4 Park Square, Milton Park, Abingdon, Oxon, OX14 4RN

Routledge is an imprint of the Taylor & Francis Group, an informa business

ISBN: 9781041161714 (hbk)
ISBN: 9781041161813 (pbk)
ISBN: 9781003683193 (ebk)

DOI: 10.4324/9781003683193

Typeset in Times New Roman
by Newgen Publishing UK

Contents

Abbreviations

AI	artificial intelligence
CEDAW	Convention on the Elimination of All Forms of Discrimination against Women
CSO	civil society organization
DEFIANCE Act	Disrupt Explicit Forged Images and Non-Consensual Edits Act
DSA	Digital Services Act
ECHR	European Convention on Human Rights
EIGE	European Institute for Gender Equality
EU	European Union
FRA	European Union Agency for Fundamental Rights
GBV	gender-based violence
GDC	Global Digital Compact
GDPR	General Data Protection Regulation
GREVIO	Group of Experts on Action against Violence against Women and Domestic Violence
ICCPR	International Covenant on Civil and Political Rights
ICT	information and communications technology
IoT	Internet of Things
NetzDG	Gesetz zur Verbesserung der Rechtsdurchsetzung in sozialen Netzwerken
NGO	non-governmental organization
PACE	Parliamentary Assembly of the Council of Europe
SDG	Sustainable Development Goals
TEU	Treaty on European Union
TFEU	Treaty on the Functioning of the European Union
TFGBV	technology-facilitated gender-based violence
UN	United Nations
UNFPA	United Nations Population Fund
VAWA	Violence against Women Act

Introduction

'It is a pity your mother did not have an abortion. Seriously. Poland would be more beautiful without such a parasite'.
'You should be shaved bald, you disgusting creature'.
'A slut betrays her country. Don't you agree with me? Because I think it is a pity that the Polish underground state does not exist today – you would be treated accordingly'.
'At least you won't have offspring and if I ever meet you, I will spit at your face with pleasure'.

Yes, I have been a victim of cyberviolence. And these are just examples of cyberviolence that I have faced on social media platforms every day while being a Deputy Commissioner for Human Rights in Poland and then a Member of the European Parliament. I have gotten rape and other sexual violence threats and 'go back to the kitchen, cunt' comments. I have been a victim of smearing, impersonalization, and disinformation campaigns.[1] And I am not the only one suffering.

Scottish First Minister, Nicola Sturgeon, faced massive online abuse, including death threats, threats of violence, and highly offensive and sexualized insults.[2] Zuzana Čaputová, Slovakian President, decided not to run for the second term after she had been subject to defamation campaigns and received death threats.[3] When Anita Sarkeesian launched a YouTube series on misogyny in video games, she received death threats and was forced to flee her home because online abusers had threatened to kill her parents, drink her blood, and rape her while publishing her personal details online.[4] Female journalists had to leave their house, region, or even country.[5]

Experiences of women in the public eye – victims of cyberviolence are described in reports and articles. And there is a nameless mass, millions of women all over the world experiencing cyberviolence on a daily basis, whose suffering and harm also deserves attention and justice. Detailed personal narratives and individual examples of experiences of cyberviolence of both public figures and individuals are extensively documented in existing reports and publications,

DOI: 10.4324/9781003683193-1

which remain valuable resources for understanding the lived experiences of victims. These accounts are not presented in this book, but readers may turn to the reports and publications referenced in the book, including reports of UNESCO, European Women's Lobby (including Anita Sarkeesian case), and Plan International (voices of girls and young women).

The Internet has changed the way we communicate, connect, and exchange information. Internet and social media platforms, in particular, have provided us with new tools and channels to work, educate, conduct our businesses, organize, take human rights actions, and defend social causes. And while women are still under-represented in public and political life, are discriminated against, and experience violence in the physical world, the Internet, technology, and digital spaces should have been tools to facilitate the achievement of gender equality. But it's quite opposite. They are often the tools to perpetuate violence, punish, control, and silence women. Mainly social media platforms are a hostile environment where not everyone is welcome, and abusers can harm women with impunity.

A new battleground has been created. Because cyberviolence against women is just a new face of an old problem – gender-based violence (GBV) that women have experienced in the physical world. Violence against women has found new tools to replicate itself. And it's serious – it's real, has severe consequences, and deprives half of the world's population of their fundamental human rights.

Addressing cyberviolence against women is no longer negotiable.[6] And it's high time to address cyberviolence against women in legislation. Because it's about the law to prevent cyberviolence, to protect the victims, and to punish the perpetrators and hold accountable all others responsible. It's about different mechanisms of civil, criminal, and administrative laws. Awareness raising (e.g., who is obliged to organize it, when and how) – is about the law, mandatory trainings (for whom, on what, how often) – is about the law, school curricula, and school books – is about the law, support services (what, where, how they should look like) – is about the law, what and how to punish – is about the law, etc.

In this book, the state of play on cyberviolence against women is presented – what we already know about the phenomenon. Chapter 1 examines what it is, what the forms of cyberviolence are, who suffer from cyberviolence and how many victims are, what the consequences are – for the victims, for the society and democracy, what the roots of cyberviolence against women are, and who the perpetrators are. In Chapter 2 we critically explore existing legal frameworks, with some examples of national laws but primarily within international and regional organizations that provide regulations for combating cyberviolence against women. In Chapter 3, a set of recommendations is proposed, brought together for the first time as a comprehensive and interdisciplinary list originating from various reports and studies and my own experience as a lawyer, human rights defender, and former Deputy Commissioner for Human Rights and Member of the European Parliament. The set of recommendations could serve as a starting point for governments to combat cyberviolence against women. It is the law that plays a significant role when it comes to influencing change in people's behaviors online as well as providing meaningful avenues of redress for women who have been subjected to cyberviolence.[7]

We need to address cyberviolence against women in legislation globally since it is a global and transnational problem. This is obvious and the recommendations concerning prevention, protection, and prosecution measures refer to global solutions and international laws. The second noticeable thing is that technology companies and social media platforms must be held accountable. Currently, as Chapter 2 shows, governments are reluctant to regulate the companies' responsibilities concerning cyberviolence perpetrated on their platforms and that they are aware of. Why? Who benefits from this? The lack of regulation is difficult to understand, especially considering the origins of one of the leading social media platforms, Facebook. Its predecessor, Facemash, aimed at comparing female students' attractiveness.[8] Internet and social media in particular produce the specific ecosystem that is an institutional space, and the digital environment is a public space[9] that can't be a lawless space.

This book does not include chapters on digital and media literacy or guidance for potential victims on how to protect themselves. Its aim is to shift the focus away from 'instructing' women on self-protection – a framing that echoes the long history of telling women how not to be raped or harassed – and instead to highlight the responsibilities of institutions and systems in ensuring safety, dignity, and equal rights within digital public spaces. The purpose of this monograph is to demonstrate the necessity of systemic change – in particular, legal reforms, and the accountability of public authorities for adopting and effectively implementing such measures – in order to guarantee safety, dignity, and equal rights in the digital sphere.

The book is based on desk research and a literature review. More than one hundred reports, surveys, and publications on cyberviolence against women were analyzed. Non-governmental organizations (NGOs) and academics, as well as human rights and equality agencies and institutions within the United Nations (UN), Council of Europe, and European Union (EU) frameworks, should be credited for their efforts to understand cyberviolence against women.

Reports, studies, and research use different terms, and they sometimes use them interchangeably, such as:

- 'information and communications technology (ICT)-facilitated violence' or 'technology-facilitated violence' – as act of violence perpetrated by one or more individuals that is committed, assisted, aggravated, and amplified in part or fully by the use of information and communication technologies or digital media, against a person on the basis of their gender;[10]
- 'online violence' – as any act of GBV against women that is committed, assisted or aggravated in part or fully by the use of ICT, such as mobile phones

and smartphones, the Internet, social media platforms, or email, against a woman because she is a woman or affects women disproportionately;[11]

- 'cyberviolence' – as an act of GBV perpetrated directly or indirectly through information and communication technologies that results in or is likely to result in, physical, sexual, psychological, or economic harm or suffering to women and girls, including threats of such acts, whether occurring in public or private life, or hindrances to the use of their fundamental rights and freedoms.[12]

Term cyberviolence against women is used in the monography. It refers to violence that takes place in cyberspace – in analogy to domestic violence, which is literally defined by the setting where it occurs, or to violence that is facilitated through cyberspace.

While the book will focus on cisgender women and girls, the references are made to the specific situation of transgender women, as the reports and research clearly state their more vulnerable position. Terms 'victims' and 'survivors' terms are used interchangeably. However, some women suffering from cyberviolence or other forms of GBV prefer to use a 'survival' term and we need to respect their preference.

I want to thank dozens of human rights experts, academics, and activists who agreed to share their views on combating cyberviolence against women. You have given me food for thought. I appreciate all discussions and meetings with my 'fellow' Fellows at the Wilson Center – thank you for all your valuable comments and ideas. Last but not least, I would like to thank the Wilson Center for giving me the opportunity to analyze one of the world's pressing challenges – gender-based cyberviolence – substantively. You were indeed a unique place for independent research, open dialogue, and actionable ideas.[13]

Notes

1 See, for example, Instytut Zamenhofa [Zamenhof Institute], 'Dezinformacja jako forma przemocy wobec kobiet w Polsce' ('Disinformation as a form of violence against women'), 2024, https://zamenhof.pl/2024/10/16/dezinformacja-jako-forma-przemocy-wobec-kobiet-w-polsce-przeczytaj-raport-instytutu-zamenhofa/ (access December 6, 2025).

2 A. Whitaker, 'Police investigating horrific catalogue of threats and abuse against Nicola Sturgeon', March 11, 2017, www.heraldscotland.com/news/15150383.police-investigating-horrific-catalogue-threats-abuse-nicola-sturgeon/ (access December 6, 2025).

3 'Slovakian president Čaputová says she will not run for re-election', June 20, 2023, www.theguardian.com/world/2023/jun/20/slovakia-president-zuzana-caputova-says-she-will-not-run-for-re-election (access December 6, 2025).

4 A. Hern, 'Feminist games critic cancels talk after terror threat', October 15, 2014, www.theguardian.com/technology/2014/oct/15/anita-sarkeesian-feminist-games-critic-cancels-talk (access December 6, 2025); J. Valenti, 'Anita Sarkeesian

interview: "The word 'troll' feels too childish. This is abuse"', August 29, 2015, www.theguardian.com/technology/2015/aug/29/anita-sarkeesian-gamergate-interv iew-jessica-valenti (access December 6, 2025).

5 UNESCO, 'The Chilling. Global trends in online violence against women journalists', 2021, https://unesdoc.unesco.org/ark:/48223/pf0000377223 (access December 6, 2025).

6 S.R. O'Brien, N.P. Fernández, '2022 Global Symposium on Technology-facilitated Gender-based Violence Results: Building a Common Pathway', Wilson Center and United Nations Population Fund (UNFPA), September 27, 2023, www.wilsoncenter.org/publication/2022-global-symposium-technology-facilitated-gender-based-viole nce-results-building (access December 6, 2025).

7 K. Barker, O. Jurasz, 'Online Misogyny as Hate Crime: A Challenge for Legal Regulation?', Routledge, 2019.

8 K.A. Kaplan, 'Facemash creator survives Ad Board', The Harvard Crimson, November 19, 2003, www.thecrimson.com/article/2003/11/19/facemash-creator-survives-ad-board-the/ (access December 6, 2025).

9 K. Ciesiołkiewicz, 'Środowisko cyfrowe – w pułapce przemocy instytucjonalnej' ('The Digital Environment – in the Trap of Institutional Violence') (in:) M. Bigaj, K. Ciesiołkiewicz, K. Mikulski, A. Miotk, J. Przewłocka, M. Rosa, A. Załęska, 'Internet dzieci. Raport z monitoringu obecności dzieci i młodzieży w internecie' ('Internet of Children. A Report on the Monitoring of the Presence of Children and Adolescents on the Internet'), Fundacja Instytut Cyfrowego Obywatelstwa (Institute for Digital Citizenship Foundation) oraz Państwowa Komisja do spraw przeciwdziałania wykorzystaniu seksualnemu małoletnich poniżej lat 15 (State Committee for Counteracting Sexual Abuse of Minors Below 15 Years of Age), 2025, https://cyfroweobywatelstwo.pl/internetdzieci/ (access September 20, 2025).

10 UNFPA, TFGBV Brochure, www.unfpa.org/sites/default/files/resource-pdf/TFGBV_Brochure-1000x560.pdf (access September 19, 2025).

11 United Nations Human Rights, 'Report of the Special Rapporteur on violence against women, its causes and consequences on online violence against women and girls from a human rights perspective', June 18, 2018, https://documents.un.org/doc/undoc/gen/g18/184/58/pdf/g1818458.pdf (access September 19, 2025).

12 Definition recommended by European Commission's Advisory Committee on Equal Opportunities for Women and Men: see European Institute for Gender Equality, 'Combating Cyber Violence against Women and Girls', November 25, 2022, https://eige.europa.eu/publications-resources/publications/combating-cyber-violence-agai nst-women-and-girls (access September 19, 2025).

13 The past tense refers to the President Donald Trump's executive order calling for the elimination of several federal entities, including the Wilson Center. The order directed the reduction of functions and personnel of the Wilson Center to the minimum required by law.

1 Cyberviolence against women

The state of play

Introduction

This chapter briefly shows what we already know about cyberviolence against women. While further research is needed on the state of play on the phenomenon of cyberviolence against women, a range of data and information is available, and NGOs and academics are leading in the efforts to understand cyberviolence against women. We present their findings and data, available in the reports and studies of the agencies, bodies, and institutions of the UN, the Council of Europe, and the EU. Based on the reports, we show the gendered nature of cyberviolence, the scale of the problem, its forms and consequences, its roots and origin, specifics of the online violence that makes it unique and 'a big deal', and what we know about the perpetrators. Last but not least, we refer to freedom of speech, an issue often raised in discussions about the safety of the Internet.

Cyberviolence as gender-based violence

In 2018, the United Nations Special Rapporteur on violence against women and girls, its causes and consequences *defined online violence against women* as any act of GBV against women that is committed, assisted, or aggravated in part or fully by the use of ICT, such as mobile phones and smartphones, the Internet, social media platforms, or email, against a woman because she is a woman, or affects women disproportionately.[1]

One could say *both women and men* can be victims of cyberviolence. However, existing research indicates that women's online experiences are different in terms of quantity and quality. Not only are women worldwide more likely than men to be attacked on the Internet, but the digital abuse they face is also specific in its nature, as it tends to be highly sexualized.[2] The forms of cyberviolence women are targeted differ from the forms of cyberviolence that are directed to men.[3] In addition, women are more likely to experience repeated and severe forms of abuse and they can suffer from serious consequences, resulting in physical, psychological, or economic harm and suffering.[4]

DOI: 10.4324/9781003683193-2

And *cyberviolence is gendered* – women and girls are targeted simply because they are women and girls.[5] It's GBV against women.[6] It reflects a similar pattern to violence against women and girls in the physical world.[7] Because just like any other form of GBV against women, cyberviolence against women is deeply rooted in the gender inequality and discrimination against women and girls that persists in the world.[8] The cyberviolence against women is an extension of the violence that has affected them for many years in all spheres of their lives.[9] Women and girls have experienced GBV in all spaces of human interaction, whether public or private, including in the contexts of the family, the community, public spaces, the workplace, leisure, politics, sport, health services, and educational settings.[10]

But first and foremost online abuse is not about image, political opinions, religious beliefs, or sexual orientation – it is about gender and is the consequence of being a woman on the Internet.[11]

Women have not been safe anywhere and now, with cyberviolence, they are not safe on the Internet, too. And the traditional system of GBV against women now uses new channels and tools. Cyberviolence against women is nothing more than a new face of an old enemy.

Numbers – how many and who?

Existing research, surveys, and studies show *the scale of the problem*. According to a study of the United Nations Broadband Commission, 73% of women experienced some form of GBV online.[12] Another global study found that 85% of women who are online witness online violence against women.[13] Country-based and regional studies also demonstrate the common nature of the problem. A survey conducted in the Arab States by UN-Women in 2021 found nearly half (49%) of women – Internet users in the region had reported feeling unsafe from online harassment.[14] The first research on cyberviolence against women conducted in 2024 in Poland, I commissioned in a public opinion survey institute, shows that almost 40% of women – Internet users in Poland – experienced cyberviolence and 64% witnessed cyberviolence against other women.[15]

The studies also show the experiences of girls and young women. The EU Agency for Fundamental Rights (FRA) found that 20% of young women (18–29) in the EU had experienced sexual cyberharassment and that 9 million European girls had experienced digital GBV by the time they were 15 years old.[16] In the United States, a survey conducted in 2014 by the Pew Research Center indicated 26% of young women (18–24) had been stalked online, and 25% had been the target of online sexual harassment.[17] According to a Plan International survey, more than half of the girls and young women experienced online violence. Forty-seven percent of girls who were harassed online were threatened with physical or sexual violence. Fifty percent of respondents reported that online harassment had been more common than street harassment.[18] The EU Kids Online survey findings showed that more girls than boys receive unwanted sexual requests online.[19]

Some research shows specific data on one of the most severe forms of cyberviolence against women – image-based sexual abuse – on the gendered nature of this type of violence. First, research indicates that up to 90% of victims of image-based sexual abuse are female.[20] Second, even 57% of women are victims of image-based sexual abuse.[21]

Women are targets because they are female but also *because of who they are and what they do.*

Cyberviolence is an *intersectional form of violence*[22] and it can be exacerbated when it is committed on the grounds of gender in combination with other factors, including age, ethnic or racial origin, sexual orientation, gender identity, disability, religion, or belief.[23] Women who have multiple identities are often targeted online on the basis of a combination of these factors and women of intersecting identities are at greater risk.[24] Certain groups of women are disproportionately disadvantaged in specific contexts. Although there is still limited data regarding the prevalence of violence and discrimination online toward certain groups, there are some figures indicating cyberviolence can be stronger toward lesbian, bisexual, intersex, and transgender women, women with disabilities, as well as women from racial minority groups, and different religious communities. The 'multiplicative effect' of cyberviolence against people from these groups can be seen.[25] Women who belong to marginalized groups receive more and qualitatively different, more intense digital pushback, given that their abuse is often intersectional.[26] For instance, as in domestic violence and sexual violence the experiences of women of color are frequently the product of intersecting patterns of racism and sexism.[27]

Globally, Plan International reported that girls and women were more likely to be harassed if they were identified as LGBTQI+, women with disabilities, women of color, or members of a minority ethnic group.[28] According to the survey of the Amnesty International, that looked at the experiences of women between the ages of 18 and 55 in Denmark, Italy, New Zealand, Poland, Spain, Sweden, the UK and USA on Twitter, women who experience multiple and intersecting forms of discrimination offline often find that violence and abuse online also targets their different identities. In the case of online violence and abuse, women of color, religious or ethnic minority women, lesbian, bisexual, transgender, or intersex (LBTI) women, women with disabilities, or non-binary individuals who do not conform to traditional gender norms of male and female often experience abuse that targets them in unique or compounded way.[29] In the United States, a Pew Research Center study shows that lesbian, gay, or bisexual adults are more likely to face harassment online.[30] Research of the Australian eSafety Commissioner indicated women with intellectual or cognitive disability could be particularly targeted to technology-facilitated violence.[31] A recent analysis of Amnesty International of the human rights implications of X's business conducted operations in Poland shows X became awash with content constituting technology-facilitated GBV, including incitement to violence, hostility, or discrimination against LGBTQI+ people and anti-LGBTQI+ content is highly prevalent on the platform.[32]

Women and girls are also the targets *because of what they do*: among them are feminist activists and feminist women and girls, female artists, women in male-dominated sectors, women human rights defenders, female journalists, members of parliaments, academics, bloggers, etc.[33]

Female journalists, bloggers, and other media actors are disproportionally experiencing gender-related threats, harassment, and intimidation on the Internet and female journalists are being coerced into silence because of the sheer volume of death threats, rape threats, threats of physical violence, and graphic imagery they receive.[34] UNESCO research on online violence against women journalists found that 73% of women journalists had experienced online violence in the course of their work, including threats of physical and sexual violence, along with digital security attacks. One in five women journalists reported that they had been abused and attacked offline in connection with online violence.[35]

Key surveys on cyberviolence against *women parliamentarians* were conducted by the Inter-Parliamentary Union. The survey, conducted in 2018 in collaboration with the Parliamentary Assembly of the Council of Europe (PACE), shown 58% of women parliamentarians had been subject to online attacks, 68% had been the target of comments relating to their physical appearance or based on gender stereotypes, and 47% had received death threats or threats of rape or beating. A study undertaken in 2021 of women parliamentarians in Africa found that 67% of those women had been subject to sexist behavior or remarks and incidents of violence had been more prevalent among women parliamentarians living with disabilities, young women under 40 years of age, unmarried women, and women from minority groups.[36]

Women activists often face pile-ons – a coordinated wave of online abuse that can include sexist comments and image-based abuse.[37] Online campaigns against women human rights defenders aim to damage their credibility as advocates, to diminish or obliterate the power of their voices, and to restrict the already limited public space in which women's activists can mobilize and make a difference.[38] Even women who 'only' participate in public Internet discussions or write about gender issues are disproportionately victims of cyberviolence. According to Amnesty International, 88% of women who use Twitter regularly for feminist debate experience abuse on the platform, and when an activist starts talking about reproductive rights issues or the Black Lives Matter movement, cyberviolence goes to a deeper level.[39] Findings from a national UK study about experiences of online abuse among women who debate feminist politics show most women experienced multiple types of abuse and almost half experienced it as a routine part of their online lives.[40] In Inter-Parliamentary Union survey conducted of women parliamentarians in 2016 more than 60% of the respondents said that taking a stance on 'controversial subjects, such as defending women's rights and human rights in general' had made them particular targets of sexist behavior and acts of violence.[41]

Behaviors and forms

There is not a commonly established *catalogue of all forms of cyberviolence* against women and girls. Existing forms constantly evolve, and new forms emerge. What is more, as UN Special Rapporteur on violence against women underlines, 'the rapid development of digital technology and spaces, including through artificial intelligence (AI), will inevitably give rise to different and new manifestations of online violence against women'.[42]

Currently, there are many forms of technology-facilitated gender-based violence (TFGBV), including but not limited to: cyberharassment, cyberstalking, hate speech,[43] image-based abuse, including non-consensual sharing of intimate images, deep fakes or sending unsolicited images of genitals or pornography to another person (sometimes called cyber-flashing), 'sextortion', gender-based slurs, 'slut-shaming', trolling, rape and death threats, 'doxing' (publishing private personal information), electronically enabled trafficking, attacks on women's groups and organizations. Many forms are interconnected or overlapping or consist of a combination of acts.[44] The behaviors should not be seen as separate, distinct events but as a spectrum of behaviors ranging from seemingly minor acts to severe forms of cyberviolence.[45]

Where women experience cyberviolence

The question of where women experience violence can be answered by one word 'everywhere'. Digital spaces where cyberviolence against women occur include social media (e.g., Facebook, X, Instagram, LinkedIn), web content and discussion/content sharing sites (e.g., Reddit), search engines (e.g., Google), messaging services (e.g., WhatsApp, Facebook Messenger, Snapchat, WeChat or Skype), blogs, dating websites and apps, comment sections of media and newspapers, forums, chat rooms of online video games, emails, text messages, etc.[46] The survey conducted in 2020 during the COVID-19 pandemic in the UK of women and non-binary individuals showed that most of the abuse had taken place on mainstream social media platforms (X, Facebook, Instagram).[47] The survey conducted in 2021 in the United States found that 75% of respondents had recently faced online abuse on social media.[48] According to a study examining the phenomenon of online violence against women across the UK, statistically X (formerly Twitter) is the platform where women and girls across the UK are most likely to experience online violence.[49]

What are the consequences and the impacts of cyberviolence against women?

Cyberviolence against women is often perceived as less severe or less harmful than offline forms of violence against women because it is 'not real', and it occurs 'only' on the Internet. But 'digital life is real life'.[50] Although more research is needed to fully understand the overall impact of cyberviolence against women, existing research shows this type of violence has serious consequences on the health, lives, and human rights of the victims as well as on society. Violence is real and similarly harms – psychological, physical, and economic ones. In the following section, we indicate only examples of research and studies showing the consequences of cyberviolence against women.

Amnesty International found that one in two women who faced online abuse or harassment experienced reduced self-esteem or loss of self-confidence, *stress, anxiety or panic attacks* because of cyber harassment. Forty-one percent of responding women online felt that their physical safety was threatened, and one in five of women in the UK (20%) and over one in four (26%) in the United States said they felt their family's safety was at risk.[51] A global study found nearly three quarters of the women surveyed expressed concern about online abuse escalating to offline threats.[52] Young women across 22 countries taking part in the survey of Plan International said that their experiences of online harassment resulted in them having lower self-esteem or losing confidence and experiencing mental or emotional stress.[53] Another research has shown survivors of cyberviolence often suffered from psychological harm, such as anxiety, depression, low self-esteem, and fear, and the psychological burden of this type of violence could lead to suicidal thoughts or suicide.[54]

The first research on female users of the Internet in Poland I commissioned in 2024 shows cyberviolence affected the private life of half of the women experiencing cyberviolence, their mental health in particular. They felt fear (49%), they lost self-confidence as their self-esteem lowered (45%). As a result of cyberviolence, one in five women experienced depression (21%), panic attacks (20%), and deterioration of health (20%); 17% of women experiencing cyberviolence reported cyberviolence affected their professional life (and 24% of those reported they had lost their income), and a similar number of women claimed their school/university life had been affected (and 13% of those women had given up education). Cyberviolence can result in the limitation of education opportunities and the deterioration of the professional and financial situation of women, increasing the risk of poverty.[55] Survivors may decide to self-regulate their online presence, preventing them from using the Internet for economic growth and business opportunities.[56] *Economic harm* can be done when the explicit image of a victim of sexual cyberabuse covers several pages of search engine results, making it difficult for the victim to find employment or even preventing the victim from attempting to find employment because of the shame and fear of potential employers discovering the images.[57]

It must be underlined that some types of cyberviolence could cause more severe consequences than others. Image-based sexual abuse is an example of such a type. Rather than experienced as a discrete incident which happens and then comes to pass, victims feel the 'constancy' of the abuse, with each new distribution or viewing being experienced as abusive, and describe the paralyzing effect it has on their daily lives. 'It can be life-ending and it is often life-shattering and leads victims to dividing their lives into 'before' and 'after' the abuse'.[58] It is probably because women are judged more harshly than men and are stigmatized for exercising their sexuality. After seeing their images distributed, they have to live in a context of permanent humiliation and shame in their social environment, which in many cases has driven them to suicide,[59] that is one of the possible physical harms experienced as a consequence of cyberviolence.

UN Special Rapporteur on violence against women and girls, its causes and consequences notes with concern that online violence against women often leads to *self-censorship* when some women resort to the use of pseudonyms, while others maintain low online profiles, decide to suspend, deactivate, or permanently delete their online accounts.[60] Amnesty International found that between 63% and 83% of women who had been harassed online changed the way they used social media, and 32% said they even stopped using it.[61] According to Plan International, 19% of the girls who were harassed very frequently used the social media less, and 12% just stopped using it.[62] Another survey shows that 41% of women between the ages of 15 and 29 self-censor to avoid online harassment.[63] British research indicates 77% of victims modified their behavior online as a result of the abuse, and 72% reported feeling differently about using technology and social media. This increased to 87% and 78%, respectively, for women of color and non-binary individuals of color.[64] Approximately 50% of women Internet users in Poland changed their patterns of online presence (they limited use of portals, accounts where a woman experienced cyberviolence, or started to use private or anonymous accounts).[65]

Further examples of this impact include *female journalists and politicians.* Nearly a third (30%) of the UNESCO survey respondents said they self-censor on social media as a result of being targeted, while 20% said they avoid all interaction online.[66] The study of the National Democratic Institute on young politically active women in Colombia, Indonesia, and Kenya that compared Twitter data with the survey responses from victims found that online abuse decreased their willingness to continue engaging in social media.[67] It should be underlined that while acts of violence against women in politics are directed at individual women, they 'have a meaning beyond their specific target: to frighten other women who are already politically active, to deter women who might consider engaging in politics, and to communicate to society that women should not participate in public life in any capacity'.[68] The YWCA and Australian University of Adelaide survey found that 80% of women over 31 and about 57% of those aged 18 to 21 were less likely to pursue their political aspirations having seen Prime Minister of Australia Julia Gillard treated negatively in the media.[69] Research of the Wilson Center revealed that online harassment campaigns cause women to reconsider and often adjust their public engagement. Women of color have increased concerns, as they receive particularly graphic, vitriolic abuse.[70] And violence and harassment should not be the cost of women's engagement in the political sphere.[71]

The UN Commission on the Status of Women acknowledges that online GBV that forces women and girls to self-censor, close their accounts on digital platforms, or reduce their interaction in online and offline spaces limits their full and meaningful participation in public life and the enjoyment of their human rights and fundamental freedoms.[72] Different UN and Council of Europe human rights frameworks entities expressed further concerns. UN Special Rapporteur on violence against women, its causes and consequences underlines online violence against women not only violates a woman's right to live free from violence and to participate online but also 'undermines democratic exercise and good governance, and as such creates a democratic deficit' by preventing women's voices from being heard freely in digital debates. Cyberviolence against women violates women's human rights as the right to a life free of violence, the right to freedom of expression and access to information, the right to privacy and protection of personal data.[73] United Nations Special Rapporteur on the promotion and protection of the right to freedom of opinion and expression emphasizes that online GBV against women is one of the most pervasive form of gendered censorship used to silence women that has serious consequences for human rights, diversity in public debates and the media, and, ultimately, democracy and development. 'Neither gender equality nor women's freedom of expression can be promoted if spaces for women to organize are not protected'. Since 'online networks are the dominant space for freedom of expression in the digital age, silencing such voices online may prevent them from being heard at all, reducing diversity and affecting democratic debate'.[74] Council of Europe Group of Experts on Action against Violence against Women and Domestic Violence (GREVIO) highlights cyberviolence against women has severe implications for women's participatory rights online, silences their voices, and reduces their perspectives in public debate.[75]

If women, girls, and marginalized communities' voices are excluded from decision-making and leadership positions – intentionally or due to trauma-related self-exclusion – then 'structural barriers such as patriarchy are solidified'. 'This withdrawal from social and public life further strengthens the dominance of male voices in already male-dominated public spheres, stifling the representation and perspectives of women, with many damaging knock-on effects'.[76] Gender-based cyberviolence makes it unsafe and unwelcoming for women and LGBTQI+ people to express themselves freely in a world where

digital communication has become one of the primary modes of communication.[77] It re-entrenches social inequalities that undermine the rights of members of equality-seeking communities to self-determination, self-representation, and dignity.[78]
As the United Nations Population Fund concludes

1 the impacts of TFGBV on mental health are severe: stress, anxiety, depression, post-complex stress disorder, suicidal ideation, and even suicide attempts;
2 when women rely on online spaces for their professional lives, cyberviolence also has serious impacts on their economic opportunities and access to resources;
3 cyberviolence silences women online and reduces their participation in public and political life, in democratic processes and leadership roles;
4 as a result, gender-based cyberviolence against women reinforces patriarchal roles, norms, and structures and is a significant barrier to gender equality.[79]

Finally, cyberviolence should be considered as a national security issue. In interviews with women targeted by Russian, Iranian, or Chinese state media, the research team of the Wilson Center study found that gendered tropes formed the basis of disinformation and smear campaigns against them.[80]

This set of impacts *generates costs* affecting victims as well as society. Some impacts can translate into economic costs, while others cannot be monetized, despite being of major relevance. The EU study estimates the overall costs of cyberharassment and cyberstalking against women at between €49 billion and €89.3 billion per year. It includes healthcare costs (reflected in an increased incidence of depression, PTSD, and anxiety disorders), legal costs, labor market costs (in terms of lower presence at work, risks of job loss, or lower productivity), and costs associated with a reduced quality of life.[81]

Not a big deal?

Cyberviolence is often *normalized, minimized and presented as a victim's fault or responsibility* mirroring the mechanisms of other forms of GBV against women, domestic violence, and sexual violence in particular. Young women and girls learn to deal with abusers, finding it 'not a big deal' or getting 'used to it'.[82] Women are generally advised to 'not feed the troll', to 'change the privacy settings', or to 'go offline for a while' and this contributes to cyberviolence being normalized.[83] Disconnecting is not a viable solution for most people in the modern world. The need for Internet connectivity is only becoming more relevant during the COVID-19 pandemic and in some countries, important public discourse, and essential governmental and civil society services are only accessible via the Internet.[84] Members of some vulnerable and marginalized groups, such as people with disability, very often rely entirely on the Internet in their education and professional lives, and disconnecting is impossible.

Despite the 'advice', *women do a lot to protect themselves online*. According to a British survey, 63% of respondents reported the abuse to social media platforms, 12% to law enforcement, 7% to NGOs, and 5% to their employer. Some 84% of respondents said their complaint had not been properly addressed, a figure which increased to 94% for Black and minoritized women and non-binary people.[85] Global survey shown many girls and young women try to tackle the harassment and reporting and blocking are used most in attempting to combat harassment. However, the respondents claim that keeping themselves safe online involves a lot of hard work.[86]

As Sarah Sobieraj writes:

> Hours and days are lost weeding through comments, Tweets, and messages. Many women invested time documenting the abuse. They organized screen shots, printed and filed materials, and otherwise worked to create a paper trail at the request of law enforcement or employers – or simply to have evidence on hand in the event of escalation. Going to court, filing reports, blocking and reporting – all these strategies sap time.[87]

Therefore, the targeted individuals might not want to report harmful content, finding the process laborious or emotionally draining, and reporting each piece of content is impractical and emotionally burdensome.[88]

Harmful content can be anywhere on the Internet, and locating content is a challenge, keeping track and documenting violence to press charges, since the evidence can disappear, be erased by perpetrators, or be unknown to the victim.[89] As in other cases of GBV, women are seen as responsible for their own safety. In case cyberviolence occurs women are seen as responsible for efficient reaction, including reporting and proving incident and harm it caused.

Women feel social media platforms and governments left the onus on targets to report and respond to harassment campaigns, and that neither were taking adequate measures, and reporting processes, and protection of targets' personal information from abusers is practically complex and emotionally exhausting.[90] Victims are responsible for regulating the attention their profiles receive and reporting abusive comments.[91] Social media platforms generally provide tools to block, mute, and otherwise restrict people from seeing somebody's posts, which allows a victim of abuse to manage their visibility and thus limits the radius of the attack. However, this 'protection' also limits the victim's ability to use the platform.[92]

As far as filing complaints is concerned, it needs to be underlined that it is very difficult for victims of GBV against women in general. In cases of online and technology-facilitated violence against women, since most law-enforcement officers are not trained to recognize the different types of violence affecting women and girls online, many of them do not know how to handle these procedures.[93] More specific legal challenges relate to law enforcement practices that risk producing further mental health strain on victims, technical challenges of accessing evidence in the online environment, and legal challenges of conducting cross-border investigations in the EU.[94] Complex, traumatic reporting mechanisms, as well as the historical oppression of vulnerable groups and fear of repercussions result in underreporting and low prosecution rates.[95]

Specific nature of cyberviolence

Cyberviolence against women is a new face of an old problem – GBV that women experience in the physical world. However, some factors make cyberviolence *particularly unique* and challenging to address. Cyberviolence:

1 is anonymous;
2 can be perpetrated at a distance;
3 is accessible and affordable for perpetrators;
4 can be automated;
5 can be constant and easily propagated;
6 can be collectively organized;
7 can be difficult to erase or remove harmful content.[96]

Technology has transformed many forms of GBV against women into something that can be perpetrated across distance, without physical contact and beyond borders through the use of anonymous profiles to amplify the harm to victims.[97] Offenders can exploit technological tools to perpetrate their abuse more efficiently and with minimal effort.[98] They can have constant access to the victim through the platforms.

Cyberviolence against women can be committed from anywhere, through a wide range of new technologies and platforms that perpetrators of violence have at their fingertips to spread permanent digital content quickly.[99] Once material has been posted, copied, re-distributed, etc., the victim's sufferings continue, though the criminal does not need to take any action.[100]

Social media and other forms of online communication allow perpetrators to work together and act simultaneously against their victims, often from different countries and time zones.[101]

In the physical world it would be impossible to recruit hundreds of men to go to an ex-girlfriend's house to demand sex but it is quite possible to arrange this via the Internet.[102]

The difficulty of permanently removing abusive content from the Internet, which obliges the survivor to re-experience their victimization all over again, is also an unprecedented characteristic of cyberviolence against women. Once data has been uploaded to a social media, the web of its shares and downloads can quickly become a labyrinth that makes removing an image's trace from the Internet a quasi-impossible task.[103] Since offensive content can be anywhere online, locating it is a challenge.[104] This is probably why young women feel that anything that happens on social media is there forever, and this makes online harassment worse.[105]

The specific nature of cyberviolence enables the perpetration of violence against women on a scale previously unknown.[106] It leads to different and unique impacts and harms compared with violence against women perpetrated in the physical world.[107]

Cyberviolence against women is *not a separate phenomenon* from violence women experience in the 'real' world. It can be a continuum of offline violence. Still, the violence can also start online and continue offline, and online and offline forms of violence against women often intersect and reinforce one another. Offline violence against women is likely to continue in online spaces and through technological means, and vice versa: abuse that starts in the digital world can turn into threats and actions of physical violence.[108] Threats and hate speech against women in public may encourage sexual or physical violence toward women and even lead to femicide. Conversely, in cases of intimate partner violence, survivors are stalked and surveilled by partners who use technology tools.[109] They monitor and track victims to control women and girls' mobility and communications.

It means different forms of violence against women and domestic violence occurring in the digital sphere and those occurring in the physical world are not mutually exclusive and frequently overlap with one another, exacerbating the traumatizing impact of the abuse. Therefore, ignoring the larger gender pattern associated with cyberviolence risks missing the social reality of violence against women stemming from the idea of the inferiority of women or stereotyped roles for women and men.[110]

In summary of the foregoing analysis, it can be argued that, on the one hand, domestic violence and cyberviolence exhibit the following similarities:

1 Power and control: In both forms, the perpetrator seeks to dominate or to punish the victim. In domestic abuse, this may mean controlling finances, movement, communication. Online, it may mean monitoring messages, impersonating the victim, threatening to release private information. And the goal is to control a woman, to show what her place is. In cyberviolence cases women are punished just for speaking out.
2 Escalation: Just as domestic violence rarely starts with physical harm, cyberviolence often escalates from 'minor' acts – mocking, name-calling – into coordinated campaigns, doxxing, threats of rape or murder.
3 Gaslighting and ignoring: In both contexts, women are often told they are overreacting and are often disbelieved. Online abuse is trivialized as 'free speech', 'jokes', or 'just the Internet'. Victims are told to ignore or log off, to stop sharing opinions.

4 Victim's blaming: In both cyber and domestic violence cases, victims are blamed. This mirrors the long history of blaming domestic violence victims – asking them why they stayed and what they did to provoke the abuser. In cyberviolence the audience asks the victim: 'Why did you post that photo? Why are you on the Internet at all?'.
5 Isolation: In domestic violence, abusers isolate victims from family and friends, from support networks. In cyberviolence they isolate women from online communities. When a woman deactivates her account, leaves a debate, or stops publishing, this is often framed as her choice – but in truth, it is a forced exit caused by persistent abuse. Victims are told to change their behavior, rather than the systems changing to protect them.
6 Institutional failure: Studies also show that women often do not report the abuse. Why? Because they do not believe anything will be done. And they're often right. Legal systems are not adapted. Law enforcement is unprepared or unwilling to respond. Whether it is the Police ignoring domestic abuse reports or platforms failing to remove harmful content, the pattern is the same – institutions minimize or ignore the violence.

On the other hand, the digital world presents unique challenges that intensify violence against women. First, the reach and speed of online abuse is unlike anything we have known before. One humiliating photo posted by primary perpetrator can be downloaded, shared, reposted endlessly from any place in the world by enormous number of secondary perpetrators.

Second, the perpetrators are often anonymous, or shielded by usernames, VPNs. This anonymity fosters a sense of impunity.

Third, the audience becomes complicit. In cyberviolence, bystanders are not neutral. When hateful content of primary abuser is liked, shared, or commented upon (be secondary ones), it gains momentum. Spectators become amplifiers.

Fourth, digital violence is invasive and inescapable. Unlike domestic violence, which often occurs in a shared physical space, cyberviolence follows women everywhere – into their homes, beds, workplaces. There is no safe offline space when the abuse is on your phone, in your inbox, on your screen.

Fifth, the legal and institutional response is fragmented and insufficient. Most countries, including the EU Member States, lack comprehensive legal frameworks to address online GBV. Platforms have inconsistent policies, and enforcement is weak. Reporting abuse is often complicated and retraumatizing. Content may be removed, but accounts remain, and if one profile is deleted, another is created.

What are the roots and goals of the cyberviolence against women?

The UN Special Rapporteur on violence against women, its causes and consequences underlines that cyberviolence against women is a reproduction of social, economic, cultural, and political structures and related forms of gender discrimination and patriarchal patterns that result in GBV against women offline. And all forms of online GBV are used to control and attack women and to maintain and reinforce patriarchal norms, roles, and structures and an unequal power relationship. This is particularly evident when violence, threats, and harassment follow speeches or expression related to gender equality and feminism, or where defenders of women's rights are targeted for their work,[111] as we indicated above.

Like any forms of GBV, cyberviolence against women has complex causes that reside in 'centuries of patriarchal norms and structures' and, as women voice their opinions online, use technology to reshape their working and personal lives or take social or political, or by simply accessing the Internet to enjoy themselves, they 'challenge an entrenched system of repression'.[112] This way cyberviolence against women is 'an extension of the history of attempts to curtail women's freedom to use public spaces as equals'.[113] Patriarchal silencing of women that takes place in offline spaces is increasingly being translated online.[114]

Research indicates the factors motivating people to perpetrate cyberviolence resemble those motivating offline GBV; 82% of the people recognize patriarchy and gender/social norms as crucial factors. Technology and online platforms are increasingly used 'as weapons to tyrannize women (and other vulnerable groups, like LGBTQI+ people), as part of an invasive 24/7 culture infiltrating workplaces, schools, and homes'.[115]

All types of violence against women have a common denominator: they are used to control, silence, and punish women, to limit women's rights, status, and opportunities. The goal and at the same time the result are to show girls and women where their place is and to keep girls and women in their place. Because women and girls both offline and online are expected to know 'their place', they are punished if they go beyond traditional 'gender order'.

Violence aims to create a hostile online environment for women to shame, intimidate, degrade, belittle, or silence women.[116] Hate speech against women online is first and foremost a corrective action which shows women users where lies the line of 'tolerable' behavior.[117]

The goal lies beyond individual women that are direct targets of cyberviolence. Women who witness cyberviolence against other women get a clear message on what is allowed and are also affected, as studies on the consequences of cyberviolence show. It means the chilling effect not only on intended targets but also on others who then avoid engaging in online spaces or even leave the spaces.

Who are the perpetrators?

Perpetrators of cyberviolence against women may be persons who are unknown to the victim, somebody in a professional circle, or even a friend or family member. A study conducted in the United States in 2017 indicated, for example, that 26% of those who have been harassed say their most recent incident involved an acquaintance, 18% – a friend, 11% – a family member, 7% – a former romantic partner, and 5% – a co-worker.[118] Since the beginning of the COVID-19 pandemic, women appear to be abused more frequently by persons who are unknown to the victim: a survey conducted during the pandemic by Glitch UK and End Violence Against Women shows that 84% of respondents experienced online abuse from strangers – accounts that they did not know before the incident(s), 16% of respondents faced abuse from an acquaintance and 10% from a partner or ex-partner, 9% of people faced abuse from a colleague or superior at work.[119]

Global survey on girls and young women conducted in 2020 shown that whilst women were listed in the examples of known harassers, none of the girls interviewed suggested women were behind the unknown accounts, many directly mentioned they thought they were men and the picture of the harasser that emerges – as survey authors claim – 'is male and conservative, from all age groups: someone particularly enraged when girls and young women speak out and do not conform to their limited ideas of femininity'.[120] Different studies confirm perpetrators of cyberviolence against women generally have a male identity. According to a study published in 2015 by the United Nations Broadband Commission for Sustainable Development, 61% of attackers were men.[121]

Two types of perpetrators of cyberviolence against women can be identified. The primary perpetrator is the person initiating the violence who first publishes harmful content. The secondary perpetrator(s) is a person or group of persons who participate in the cyberviolence after the initial act of cyberviolence and forwards, shares, or reposts harmful content.[122]

A list of 12 different types of abusers, with their habitat and their tactics, was prepared by the European Women's Lobby (EWL), the European umbrella network of women's organizations.[123] The EWL indicates there are different types of perpetrators and they use different platforms. Perpetrators can be relatives or acquaintances of the victim: (ex-)intimate partners, school/college classmates, co-workers, but also online criminals like impersonators and hackers. Perpetrators can have a political or religious motive or agenda, as in the case of groups opposing women's rights or targeting women's participation. Lastly, individuals and organized groups including sexual predators, traffickers, pedophilic networks, and transnational criminal organizations are among categories of perpetrators.

The list of cyberviolence perpetrators includes the following:

1 the troll/the cyber sexual harasser. Tactics: Attacks women who assert their opinions online. Habitat: Comments sections, forums, chat rooms;
2 the creepshotter/the digital voyeur and violator. Tactics: Photographs women and girls without their consent and publishes their photos online. Habitat: Offline public places, Reddit, dedicated websites, social networks;

3 the image-based sexual abuser[124]/the digital rapist. Tactics: Posts private pictures or videos of a sexual nature to shame and humiliate the victim. Extension of intimate partner violence. Habitat: Social networks;
4 the online groomer/the child sexual abuser. Tactics: Builds a relationship with a child via the Internet to bring them into sexual abuse/sex trafficking. Habitat: Social networks, forums;
5 the cyberstalker/the obsessive abuser. Tactics: Spies, fixates on, and compiles information about women online to scare them and blackmail them. Habitat: Social networks;
6 the masculinist/the woman hater. Tactics: Negates and though perpetuates systemic sexism by 'defending men's rights'. Habitat: Dedicated websites, women's groups' websites, social networks;
7 the cyberbully/the humiliator. Tactics: Repeatedly sends hurtful messages and starts rumors to shame and humiliate. Habitat: Social networks, communication apps;
8 the dating website manipulator/the sexual predator. Tactics: Seeks power and control over their victim by charming them online and luring them toward a dangerous situation. Habitat: Dating websites, social networks, chat rooms, communication apps;
9 the recruiter/the rape seller aka the trafficker. Tactics: Uses new technologies to lure victims, traffic, and sell them, and prostitute them. Habitat: Sales websites, dedicated platforms, social media, communication apps;
10 the doxxer/the data thief and criminal shamer. Tactics: Researches and publishes private information online to publicly expose and shame victims. Habitat: Victim's social networks profiles, Google searches;
11 the malicious distributor/the dangerous defamatory. Tactics: Uses new technologies and a propaganda tool to promote violence against women or women's rights groups. Habitat: Social networks;
12 the hacker/the invader. Tactics: Intercepts private information and communication, i.e. webcams. Habitat: Can be everywhere.[125]

Free speech?

Last, we need to address two issues that raise questions, doubts, and controversies in almost every debate on the safety of digital spaces and the protection of victims of cyberviolence.

The first one is an issue of *anonymity*. As UN Special Rapporteur on violence against women, its causes and consequences underlines, anonymity online is an important role for women and others at risk of discrimination and stigma, in that 'it allows them to seek information, find solidarity and support and share opinions without fear of being identified. This holds particularly true for individuals who face discrimination and persecution based on their sexual orientation and gender identity'.[126] However, it's again the position of the Special Rapporteur on violence against women, its causes and consequences, 'while preserving anonymity for users is essential, the identification of perpetrators is necessary if online gender-based violence is to be addressed'.[127] We couldn't agree more.

The second issue is *freedom of speech*. As shown in this chapter, cyberviolence deprives women and other people from marginalized groups of opportunities to express themselves on social media and the Internet. Cyberviolence violates their freedom of speech, while on the other side perpetrators and abusers seem to hold 'freedom of hate speech' instead of freedom of speech. However, there is no 'freedom of hate speech' in the fundamental rights and freedoms catalog. 'Freedom of hate speech' is not protected nor guaranteed. In addition, under the international human rights framework, governments have a positive obligation to create an environment in which all can participate in public debate without fear. Thus, 'censorship' of online hate speech is necessary to protect the free speech of others.[128] Undoubtedly, the question of freedom of speech should be raised. The crucial questions are not just whether the right balance is struck between freedom of expression and protecting marginalized groups from hate speech, but rather:

1 whose freedom of expression is protected;[129]
2 whose rights are being prioritized and whose voices are silenced;[130]
3 is hiding behind the concept of freedom of expression taking the perpetrator's side?

Conclusions

The collection of the reports, research, and studies shows cyberviolence is GBV against women. It's an everyday experience of many women and girls, because they are female and they are online. It severely affects their health, lives, and the future. Such as in the case of violence against women, offline, cyberviolence against women is aimed at controlling, silencing, and punishing women. These goals are often met since women start to self-censor themselves after experiencing cyberviolence or 'only' witness online violence against other women. Such as in offline forms of violence, women are considered to be responsible for their own safety on the Internet and are blamed if cyberviolence occurs. But some unique factors of cyberviolence make it even more challenging to deal with than offline violence against women. While cyberviolence is often minimized and normalized, it is 'a big deal'. It's about individual harm but also human rights and democracy. It's also about spending a lot of money because the system doesn't protect women from cyberviolence. Because of all of that, it's high time to address it in the legislation in an efficient way to protect victims, punish perpetrators, and hold accountable all others responsible.

Notes

1 United Nations Human Rights, 'Report of the special rapporteur on violence against women, its causes and consequences on online violence against women and girls from a human rights perspective', June 18, 2018, https://documents.un.org/doc/undoc/gen/g18/184/58/pdf/g1818458.pdf See also similar definitions of UN Women in 'Accelerating efforts to tackle online and technology facilitated violence against women and girls (VAWG)', 2022, www.unwomen.org/sites/default/files/2022-10/Accelerating-efforts-to-tackle-online-and-technology-facilitated-violence-against-women-and-girls-en_0.pdf (access December 6, 2025); UNFPA, TFGBV Brochure www.unfpa.org/sites/default/files/resource-pdf/TFGBV_Brochure-1000x560.pdf; EU directive on combating violence against women and domestic violence: https://eur-lex.europa.eu/eli/dir/2024/1385/oj/eng

2 GenPol – Gender & Policy Insights, 'When Technology Meets Misogyny. Multi-level, Intersectional Solutions to Digital Gender-Based Violence', 2020, https://www.thewomensorganisation.org.uk/wp-content/uploads/2020/09/When-Technology-Meets-Misogyny-GenPol-Policy-Paper-2.pdf (access December 6, 2025).

3 M. Duggan, 'Online Harassment', Pew Research Center, October 22, 2014, www.pewinternet.org/2014/10/22/online-harassment/ (access December 6, 2025) and similarly – a survey conducted 7 years later: E.A. Vogels, 'The state of online harassment', January 13, 2021, Pew Research Center, www.pewresearch.org/wp-content/uploads/sites/20/2021/01/PI_2021.01.13_Online-Harassment_FINAL-1.pdf (access December 6, 2025).

4 Group of Experts on Action against Violence against Women and Domestic Violence (GREVIO), 'GREVIO General Recommendation No. 1 on the digital dimension of violence against women', October 20, 2021, https://rm.coe.int/grevio-rec-no-on-digital-violence-against-women/1680a49147 (access December 6, 2025); European Parliament's Policy Department for Citizens' Rights and Constitutional Affairs, 'The impact of the use of social media on women and girls', March 2023, www.europarl.europa.eu/RegData/etudes/STUD/2023/743341/IPOL_STU(2023)743341_EN.pdf (access December 6, 2025).

5 UNFPA, TFGBV Brochure, www.unfpa.org/sites/default/files/resource-pdf/TFGBV_Brochure-1000x560.pdf

6 Gender-based violence against women is currently used as a more precise term that makes explicit the gendered causes and impacts of the violence, CEDAW Committee, 'General recommendation No. 35 (2017) on gender-based violence against women, updating general recommendation No. 19 (1992)', July 26, 2017, www.ohchr.org/en/documents/general-comments-and-recommendations/general-recommendation-no-35-2017-gender-based (access September 19, 2025); see also reference to General recommendation No. 35 and General recommendation No. 19 in Chapter 2.

7 United Nations, General Assembly, 'Intensification of efforts to eliminate all forms of violence against women and girls. Report of the Secretary General', August 18, 2022, https://documents.un.org/doc/undoc/gen/n22/465/68/pdf/n2246568.pdf (access December 6, 2025).

8 European Institute for Gender Equality, 'Combating cyber violence against women and girls', November 25, 2022, https://eige.europa.eu/publications-resources/publications/combating-cyber-violence-against-women-and-girls
9 Organization of American States: Inter-American Committee against Terrorism (CICTE), Inter-American Commission of Women (CIM), 'Online gender-based violence against women and girls. Guide of basic concepts', 2021, www.oas.org/en/sms/cicte/docs/Guide-basic-concepts-Online-gender-based-violence-against-women-and-girls.pdf (access December 6, 2025).
10 CEDAW Committee, 'General recommendation No. 35 (2017) on gender-based violence against women, updating general recommendation No. 19 (1992)', July 26, 2017, www.ohchr.org/en/documents/general-comments-and-recommendations/general-recommendation-no-35-2017-gender-based.
11 S. Watson, 'Online abuse of women: an interdisciplinary scoping review of the literature', Feminist Media Studies 2024/24(1), pp. 1–19, https://doi.org/10.1080/14680777.2023.2181136.
12 United Nations Broadband Commission for Digital Development, Working Group on Broadband and Gender, 'Cyber Violence against Women and Girls. A world-wide wake-up call', October 23, 2015, www.broadbandcommission.org/publication/cyber-violence-against-women/ (access December 6, 2025).
13 The Economist Intelligence Unit, 'Measuring the prevalence of online violence against women', March 1, 2021, https://onlineviolencewomen.eiu.com/ (access December 6, 2025).
14 UN-Women, Arab States, 'Violence against women in the online space: insights from a multi-country study in the Arab States', 2021, https://arabstates.unwomen.org/en/digital-library/publications/2021/11/violence-against-women-in-the-online-space (access December 6, 2025).
15 S. Spurek, 'Cyberprzemoc wobec kobiet w Polsce. Raport z badań' ('Cyberviolence against women in Poland. Survey report'), 2024, https://sylwiaspurek.pl/ (access December 6, 2025).
16 European Union Agency for Fundamental Rights, 'Violence against women: an EU-wide survey. Results at a glance', 2014, https://fra.europa.eu/sites/default/files/fra-2014-vaw-survey-at-a-glance-oct14_en.pdf (access December 6, 2025).
17 M. Duggan, 'Online Harassment', Pew Research Center, October 22, 2014, www.pewinternet.org/2014/10/22/online-harassment/.
18 Plan International, 'State of the World's Girls 2020: Free to Be Online. A report on girls' and young women's experiences of online harassment', 2020, https://plan-international.org/publications/free-to-be-online/ (access December 6, 2025).
19 D. Smahel, H. Machackova, G. Mascheroni, L. Dedkova, E. Staksrud, K. Ólafsson, S. Livingstone, U Hasebrink., 'EU Kids Online 2020: Survey results from 19 countries', EU Kids Online, London School of Economics and Political Science, 2020, https://eprints.lse.ac.uk/103294/ (access September 25, 2025).
20 Cyber Civil Rights Initiative, 'End Revenge Porn. A Campaign of the Cyber Civil Rights Initiative, Inc.', www.cybercivilrights.org/wp-content/uploads/2014/12/RPStatistics.pdf (access December 6, 2025).
21 The Economist Intelligence Unit, 'Measuring the prevalence of online violence against women', March 1, 2021, https://onlineviolencewomen.eiu.com/.

22 The term intersectionality references the critical insight that race, class, gender, sexuality, ethnicity, nation, ability, and age operate not as unitary, mutually exclusive entities, but rather as reciprocally constructing phenomena; see P.H. Collins, 'Intersectionality's Definitional Dilemmas', Annual Review of Sociology 2015/41(1).

23 European Institute for Gender Equality, 'Combating cyber violence'; Organization of American States, Inter-American Committee against Terrorism (CICTE), Inter-American Commission of Women (CIM), 'Online gender-based violence'. On disability hate speech online, see M. Sherry, T. Olsen, J.S. Vedele, 'Disability Hate Speech: Social, Cultural and Political Contexts', Routledge, 2019. The authors claim that new technologies have not simply allowed online prejudice to move into new arenas – the very nature and content of such prejudices have changed and new discourses of hatred and new forms of harassment emerge online (such as cyberbullying, online harassment, doxxing, swatting, cyberstalking, and trolling).

24 United Nations Human Rights, 'Report of the Special Rapporteur'; A. van der Wilk, 'Protecting women and girls from violence in the digital age. The relevance of the Istanbul Convention and the Budapest Convention on Cybercrime in addressing online and technology-facilitated violence against women', Council of Europe, 2021, https://edoc.coe.int/en/violence-against-women/10686-protecting-women-and-girls-from-violence-in-the-digital-age.html (access December 6, 2025).

25 European Parliamentary Research Service, 'Combating gender-based violence: Cyber violence. European added value assessment', March 2021, www.europarl.europa.eu/RegData/etudes/STUD/2021/662621/EPRS_STU(2021)662621_EN.pdf (access December 6, 2025); European Union Agency for Fundamental Rights, 'Challenges to women's human rights in the EU. Gender discrimination, sexist hate speech and gender-based violence against women and girls', November 2017, https://fra.europa.eu/sites/default/files/fra_uploads/fra-2017-challenges-to-women-human-rights_en.pdf (access December 6, 2025).

26 S. Sobieraj, 'Credible Threat: Attacks against Women Online and the Future of Democracy', Oxford University Press, 2020, p. 97.

27 K. Crenshaw, 'Mapping the Margins: Intersectionality, Identity Politics, and Violence against Women of Color', Stanford Law Review 1991/43(6).

28 Plan International, 'State of the world's girls 2020'.

29 Amnesty International, '#ToxicTwitter. Violence and abuse against women online', 2018, www.amnestyusa.org/wp-content/uploads/2018/03/Toxic-Twitter.pdf (access December 6, 2025).

30 Vogels, 'The state'.

31 eSafety Commissioner of Australia, '"For my safety". Experiences of technology-facilitated abuse among women with intellectual disability or cognitive disability', August 2021, www.esafety.gov.au/sites/default/files/2021-09/TFA%20WWICD_accessible.pdf (access December 6, 2025).

32 Amnesty International, 'Poland: "A Thousand Cuts" technology-facilitated gender-based violence against Poland's LGBTI community on X', September 1, 2025, www.amnesty.org/en/documents/eur37/0098/2025/en/ (access September 20, 2025).

33 See, for example, online violence against women and girls in sports in K. Barker, O. Jurasz, '#MeToo, sport, and women: foul, own goal, or touchdown? Online abuse of women in sport as a contemporary issue', (in:) 'Sports and Human Rrights', eds.

V. Boillet, S. Weerts, A.R. Ziegler, Springer, 2024. The study investigates the prevalence of cyberbullying among university faculty shows that female faculty members are disproportionately targeted with gendered forms of cyberbullying, L.R. Salazar, A. Amores-Villalba, E. Larrañaga, S. Yubero, R. Navarro, 'Cyberbullying of university faculty: An examination of gender differences in cyberbullying victimization in higher education', Computers in Human Behavior 2024/155(C).

34 Organization for Security and Cooperation in Europe (OSCE), Representative on Freedom of the Media, 'New Challenges to Freedom of Expression. Countering Online Abuse of Female Journalists', 2016, www.osce.org/files/f/documents/c/3/220411.pdf (access December 6, 2025).

35 UNESCO, 'The Chilling. Global trends in online violence against women journalists', 2021, https://unesdoc.unesco.org/ark:/48223/pf0000377223 (access December 6, 2025).

36 Inter-Parliamentary Union, 'Sexism, harassment and violence against women in parliaments in Africa', 2021, www.ipu.org/resources/publications/issue-briefs/2021-11/sexism-harassment-and-violence-against-women-in-parliaments-in-africa (access December 6, 2025).

37 World Wide Web Foundation, 'Online gender-based violence and abuse: Consultation briefing', 2021, https://uploads-ssl.webflow.com/61557f76c8a63ae527a819e6/615585a9bbfeb8836d512947_OGBV_ConsultationBriefing.pdf (access December 6, 2025).

38 United Nations Human Rights, 'The Impact of online violence on women human rights defenders and women's organisations', June 21, 2018, www.ohchr.org/en/statements/2018/06/impact-online-violence-women-human-rights-defenders-and-womens-organisations (access December 6, 2025).

39 Amnesty International, '#ToxicTwitter'.

40 R. Lewis, M. Rowe, C. Wiper, 'Online Abuse of Feminists as An Emerging form of Violence Against Women and Girls', The British Journal of Criminology 2017/57(6).

41 Inter-Parliamentary Union, 'Sexism, harassment'.

42 United Nations Human Rights, 'Report of the Special Rapporteur'.

43 See defining the sexist hate speech term in K. Sękowska-Kozłowska, G. Baranowska, A. Gliszczyńska-Grabias, 'Sexist hate speech and the international human rights law. Towards legal recognition of the phenomenon by the United Nations and the Council of Europe', International Journal of the Semiotics of Law 2022/35, p. 2323–2345, https://doi.org/10.1007/s11196-022-09884-8 (access December 6, 2025); on text-based abuse see O. Jurasz, K. Barker, 'Online text-based (sexual) abuse', (in:) 'Gender-based violence. A comprehensive guide', eds. P. Ali, M. Rogers, Springer, 2023, https://doi.org/10.1007/978-3-031-05640-6_38 (access December 6, 2025).

44 See more on terminology in the reports of the UN, Council of Europe and the European Union including: UNFPA, TFGBV Brochure; A. van der Wilk, 'Protecting women and girls'; Cybercrime Convention Committee (T-CY), Working Group on cyberbullying and other forms of online violence, especially against women and children, 'Mapping study on cyberviolence', July 9, 2018, https://rm.coe.int/t-cy-2017-10-cbg-study-provisional/16808c4914 (access November 21, 2024); Council of Europe, 'Types of cyberviolence', www.coe.int/en/web/cyberviolence/types-of-cyberviolence (access December 6, 2025); European Institute for Gender Equality, 'Combating Cyber Violence'; European Parliamentary Research Service, 'Combating

gender-based violence'; European Parliament, Policy Department for Citizens' Rights and Constitutional Affairs, 'Cyber violence and hate speech online against women', September 2018, www.europarl.europa.eu/RegData/etudes/STUD/2018/604979/IPOL_STU(2018)604979_EN.pdf (access December 6, 2025). An examples on how women's human rights organizations and their employees experienced online threats by fundamentalist paramilitary groups – see the Association for Progressive Communications, 'End violence case studies', 2015, www.genderit.org/articles/protecting-right-freedom-expression-strategies-survivors-tech-related-violence-against (access December 6, 2025). The concept of semiotic violence against women should be mentioned that is violence perpetrated through degrading images and sexist language, M.L. Krook, 'Semiotic Violence against Women: Theorizing Harms against Female Politicians', Journal of Women in Culture and Society 2022/47(2). The semiotic violence could be related to many manifestations of cyberviolence against women.

45 Liz Kelly's influential concept of the continuum of sexual violence demonstrates that violence against women cannot be reduced to discrete incidents, and all of these practices are connected by the same underlying structures of power and control. This framework is highly relevant for the digital sphere: online abuse mirrors this continuum, extending from everyday microaggressions such as sexist jokes, memes, or derogatory comments, through persistent harassment and threats, to the most extreme forms of technology-facilitated violence, including cyberstalking, doxing, and image-based sexual abuse. L. Kelly, 'Surviving Sexual Violence', Cambridge: Polity Press, 1988.

46 See, for example, European Parliament, Policy Department for Citizens' Rights and Constitutional Affairs, 'Cyber violence and hate speech'.

47 End Violence against Women Coalition and Glitch UK, 'The ripple effect. COVID-19 and the epidemic of online abuse', 2020, www.endviolenceagainstwomen.org.uk/online-abuse-during-covid-almost-half-of-women-have-experienced-online-abuse-during- (access December 6, 2025).

48 Vogels, 'The state'.

49 O. Jurasz, 'Online violence against women: A Four Nations study', The Open University, 2024, https://oro.open.ac.uk/96398/ (access December 6, 2025).

50 UNFPA, TFGBV Brochure.

51 Amnesty International, '#ToxicTwitter'.

52 The Economist Intelligence Unit, 'Measuring the prevalence'.

53 Plan International, 'State of the World's Girls 2020'.

54 Generation G partnership, 'Decoding technology-facilitated gender-based violence: a reality check from seven countries', 2024, https://rutgers.international/resources/decoding-technology-facilitated-gender-based-violence-a-reality-check-from-seven-countries/ (access December 6, 2025).

55 S. Spurek, 'Cyberprzemoc wobec kobiet' ('Cyberviolence against women').

56 Generation G partnership, 'Decoding technology-facilitated gender-based violence'.

57 United Nations Human Rights, 'Report of the Special Rapporteur'.

58 C. McGlynn *et al.*, 'It's Torture for the soul. The harms of image-based sexual abuse', Social & Legal Studies 2021/30(4), p. 541–562, https://doi.org/10.1177/0964663920947791 (access December 6, 2025); C. Rigotti, C. McGlynn, 'Towards an EU criminal law on violence against women: The ambitions and limitations of the Commission's proposal to criminalize image-based sexual abuse', New Journal

of European Criminal Law 2022/13(4), p. 452–477, https://doi.org/10.1177/20322844221140713 (access December 6, 2025).

59 Organization of American States: Inter-American Committee against Terrorism (CICTE), Inter-American Commission of Women (CIM), 'Online gender-based violence'.

60 United Nations Human Rights, 'Report of the Special Rapporteur'.

61 Amnesty International, '#ToxicTwitter'.

62 Plan International, 'State of the World's Girls 2020'.

63 A. Lenhart *et al.*, 'Online harassment, digital abuse, and cyberstalking in America', Data & Society, November 21, 2016, https://datasociety.net/library/online-harassment-digital-abuse-cyberstalking/ (access December 6, 2025).

64 End Violence against Women Coalition and Glitch UK, 'The ripple effect'.

65 S. Spurek, 'Cyberprzemoc wobec kobiet' ('Cyberviolence against women').

66 UNESCO, 'The Chilling'.

67 National Democratic Institute, 'Tweets that chill. Analyzing online violence against women in politics. Report of case study research in Indonesia, Colombia, and Kenya', 2019, www.ndi.org/sites/default/files/NDI%20Tweets%20That%20Chill%20Report.pdf (access December 6, 2025).

68 National Democratic Institute, '#NotTheCost. Stopping violence against women in politics. A Call to Action', 2016, www.ndi.org/sites/default/files/1%20%23NotTheCost%20-%20Call%20to%20Action.pdf (access December 6, 2025).

69 T. Shepherd, 'More women turning off politics after Julia Gillard was badly treated', The Advertiser, January 14, 2014, www.adelaidenow.com.au/news/south-australia/more-women-turning-off-politics-after-julia-gillard-was-badly-treated/news-story/321177664cf100e0316704bad5c5f8a6 (access December 6, 2025).

70 N. Jankowicz *et al.*, 'Malign creativity. How gender, sex, and lies are weaponized against women online', Wilson Center, January 2021, www.wilsoncenter.org/sites/default/files/media/uploads/documents/Report%20Malign%20Creativity%20How%20Gender%2C%20Sex%2C%20and%20Lies%20are%20Weaponized%20Against%20Women%20Online_0.pdf (access December 6, 2025).

71 M.L. Krook, J. Restrepo Sanín, 'The Cost of Doing Politics? Analyzing Violence and Harassment against Female Politicians', Perspectives on Politics 2020/18(3).

72 Commission on the Status of Women, CSW67 Agreed Conclusions, 'Innovation and technological change, and education in the digital age for achieving gender equality and the empowerment of all women and girls', 67. Session, March 6–7, 2023, https://documents.un.org/doc/undoc/ltd/n23/081/71/pdf/n2308171.pdf (access December 6, 2025).

73 United Nations Human Rights, 'Report of the Special Rapporteur'.

74 United Nations Human Rights, 'A/76/258: Gender justice and freedom of expression – Report of the Special Rapporteur on the promotion and protection of the right to freedom of opinion and expression on gender justice and freedom of opinion and expression', July 30, 2021, www.ohchr.org/en/documents/thematic-reports/a76258-gender-justice-and-freedom-expression-report-special-rapporteur (access December 6, 2025).

75 Group of Experts on Action against Violence against Women and Domestic Violence (GREVIO), 'GREVIO General Recommendation No. 1'.

76 Generation G partnership, 'Decoding technology-facilitated gender-based violence'.

77 S. Dunn, 'Technology-Facilitated Gender-Based Violence: An Overview', December 7, 2020, www.cigionline.org/publications/technology-facilitated-gender-based-violence-overview/ (access December 6, 2025).

78 J. Bailey, J. Burkell, S. Dunn, Ch. Gosse, V. Steeves, 'AI and Technology-Facilitated Violence and Abuse', (in:) 'Artificial Intelligence and the Law in Canada', eds. F. Martin-Bariteau, T. Scassa, Toronto: LexisNexis Canada, 2021, https://ssrn.com/abstract=3734663 (access February 19, 2025).

79 UNFPA, TFGBV Brochure.

80 N. Jankowicz *et al.*, 'Malign creativity'.

81 The wide range reflects the underlying uncertainty concerning the prevalence of cyberharassment and cyberstalking experienced by women in the EU, European Parliamentary Research Service, 'Combating gender-based violence'.

82 Plan International, 'State of the World's Girls 2020'.

83 European Parliament, Policy Department for Citizens' Rights and Constitutional Affairs, 'Cyber violence and hate speech'.

84 S. Dunn, 'Technology-Facilitated Gender-Based Violence'.

85 End Violence against Women Coalition and Glitch UK, 'The ripple effect'.

86 Plan International, 'State of the World's Girls 2020'.

87 S. Sobieraj, 'Credible Threat', p. 110.

88 European Parliament, Policy Department for Citizens' Rights and Constitutional Affairs, 'Social media platforms and challenges for democracy, rule of law and fundamental rights', April 2023, www.europarl.europa.eu/RegData/etudes/STUD/2023/743400/IPOL_STU(2023)743400_EN.pdf (access December 6, 2025).

89 A. van der Wilk, 'Protecting women and girls'.

90 N. Jankowicz *et al.*, 'Malign creativity'.

91 European Parliamentary Research Service, 'Combating gender-based violence'.

92 UNESCO, 'Your opinion doesn't matter, anyway. Exposing technology-facilitated gender-based violence in an era of generative AI', 2023, https://unesdoc.unesco.org/ark:/48223/pf0000387483 (access December 6, 2025).

93 A. van der Wilk, 'Protecting women and girls'.

94 European Parliamentary Research Service, 'Combating gender-based violence'.

95 Generation G partnership, 'Decoding technology-facilitated gender-based violence'.

96 UNFPA, TFGBV Brochure.

97 United Nations Human Rights, 'Report of the Special Rapporteur'.

98 R. de Silva de Alwis, 'A Rapidly Shifting Landscape. Why Digitized Violence is the Newest Category of Gender-Based Violence', La Revue des Juristes de Sciences Po 2024/25, p. 62, U of Penn Law School, Public Law Research Paper No. 23–43, https://ssrn.com/abstract=4618409 (access December 6, 2025).

99 Organization of American States: Inter-American Committee Against Terrorism (CICTE), Inter-American Commission of Women (CIM), 'Online gender-based violence'.

100 Cybercrime Convention Committee (T-CY), Working Group on cyberbullying and other forms of online violence, especially against women and children, 'Mapping study'.

101 GenPol – Gender & Policy Insights, 'When Technology Meets Misogyny'.

102 Cybercrime Convention Committee (T-CY), Working Group on cyberbullying and other forms of online violence, especially against women and children, 'Mapping study'.

103 GenPol – Gender & Policy Insights, 'When Technology Meets Misogyny'.
104 European Parliament, Policy Department for Citizens' Rights and Constitutional Affairs, 'Cyber violence and hate speech'.
105 Plan International, 'State of the World's Girls 2020'.
106 Group of Experts on Action against Violence against Women and Domestic Violence (GREVIO), 'GREVIO General Recommendation No. 1'.
107 European Institute for Gender Equality, 'Combating Cyber Violence'.
108 UNFPA, 'Technology-facilitated Gender-based Violence: Making all spaces safe', December 1, 2021, www.unfpa.org/publications/technology-facilitated-gender-based-violence-making-all-spaces-safe (access December 6, 2025).
109 S.R. O'Brien, N.P. Fernández, '2022 Global Symposium on technology-facilitated gender-based violence results: building a common pathway', *Wilson Center and UNFPA*, September 27, 2023, www.wilsoncenter.org/publication/2022-global-symposium-technology-facilitated-gender-based-violence-results-building.
110 Group of Experts on Action against Violence against Women and Domestic Violence (GREVIO), 'GREVIO General Recommendation No. 1'.
111 United Nations Human Rights, 'Report of the Special Rapporteur'.
112 GenPol – Gender & Policy Insights, 'When Technology Meets Misogyny'.
113 S. Sobieraj, 'Credible Threat', p. 4.
114 Digital Rights Foundation, 'Policy paper. Perspectives on gender disinformation', 2021, https://digitalrightsfoundation.pk/work/research/ (access December 6, 2025); see also L. Giugni, 'The Threat: Why Digital Capitalism is Sexist. And How to Resist', September Publishing, 2022; E. Siapera, 'Online misogyny as witch hunt: primitive accumulation in the age of techno-capitalism', (in:) 'Gender hate online', eds. D. Ging, E. Siapera, Palgrave Macmillan, 2019, https://doi.org/10.1007/978-3-319-96226-9_2 (access December 6, 2025).
115 Generation G partnership, 'Decoding technology-facilitated gender-based violence'.
116 Amnesty International, '#ToxicTwitter'.
117 L. Richardson-Self, 'Hate Speech against Women Online. Concepts and Countermeasures', Lanham, 2021, p. 3.
118 M. Duggan, 'Online Harassment', Pew Research Center, July 11, 2017, www.pewresearch.org/internet/2017/07/11/online-harassment-2017/ (access December 6, 2025).
119 End Violence against Women Coalition and Glitch UK, 'The ripple effect'.
120 Plan International, 'State of the World's Girls 2020'.
121 United Nations Broadband Commission for Digital Development, Working Group on Broadband and Gender, 'Cyber Violence against Women and Girls'; see also A. van der Wilk, 'Protecting women and girls'.
122 Z. Abdul Aziz, 'Due diligence and accountability for online violence against women', July 31, 2017, www.apc.org/en/pubs/due-diligence-and-accountability-online-violence-against-women (access December 6, 2025).
123 European Women's Lobby, '#HerNetHerRights. Mapping the state of online violence against women and girls in Europe', 2017, www.womenlobby.org/IMG/pdf/hernetherrights_report_2017_for_web.pdf (access December 6, 2025).
124 Original list refers to 'the revenge pornographer' term that we avoid to use in the book as it doesn't reflect the nature and all aspects of image-based sexual abuse.
125 European Women's Lobby, '#HerNetHerRights'.

126 United Nations Human Rights, 'Report of the Special Rapporteur'.
127 United Nations Human Rights, 'Report of the Special Rapporteur'.
128 European Parliament, Policy Department for Citizens' Rights and Constitutional Affairs, 'Social media platforms'. And undoubtedly fact-checking doesn't censor free speech, P.M. Barrett, 'Some Facts About Fact-Checking: Defending the Imperfect Search for Truth in an Era of Institutionalized Lying', January 27, 2025, www.techpolicy.press/some-facts-about-fact-checking-defending-the-imperfect-search-for-truth-in-an-era-of-institutionalized-lying/ (access February 02, 2025).
129 European Parliament, Policy Department for Citizens' Rights and Constitutional Affairs, 'Social media platforms'.
130 Plan International 'State of the World's Girls 2020'.

2 Cyberviolence against women

Legal landscapes

Introduction

The findings presented in the Chapter 1 show the system doesn't protect women from cyberviolence. Ideally, the first and the last recourse available for women experiencing cyberviolence should be self-regulations of the platforms, and there should be no need to execute national or international binding laws. However, self-regulations

> are created by cisgender white men for users like themselves. As a result, they often fail to imagine the myriad and unique attacks which abusers employ against women and people of color in the public sphere, as well as the effect these attacks have on their targets.[1]

Research and studies show that social media platforms don't take adequate measures to protect online safety and don't exact meaningful consequences for perpetrators.[2] The platforms don't do enough to address online abuse, and too often no action is taken. Replies from social media companies are usually non-existent, unhelpful, and come too late.[3] Major social media companies do not appear capable of reliably and effectively enforcing their stated policies.[4] The first Polish research on cyberviolence against women indicates 16% of victims were informed by social media platforms that the reported content did not breach community standards, 12% – that a reported profile was compliant with community standards, and 17% of respondents didn't get any response to their notification.[5] Eighty-three percent of respondents support the opinion that platforms should fight cyberviolence, and 67% believe that liability for cyberviolence and hate speech should be imposed on social media portals and Internet platforms; 81% of women – Internet users in Poland clearly see the need to implement laws to protect victims of cyberviolence effectively.[6] European Union Agency for Fundamental Rights (FRA), an EU body tasked with collecting and analyzing data on fundamental rights, underlines that social media content moderation systems fail to correctly identify some posts that could constitute online hate,

DOI: 10.4324/9781003683193-3

especially misogyny.[7] The degree of misogyny found during the FRA research on online content moderation indicates that both regulators and online platforms should strengthen their efforts to ensure a safer and non-discriminatory environment for women online, including more targeted legal action. The volume of potential misogyny that has slipped through the platforms' online content moderation indicates that discrimination against women – in the form of online hate – is inherent in the algorithms, as they fail to pick up this form of content.[8]

As the UN Commission on the Status of Women underlines the way many digital platforms are designed, maintained, and governed has given rise to disinformation, misinformation, and hate speech, which can undermine the fulfillment of women's and girls' rights, including the right to freedom of opinion and expression and to participate in all spheres of public life.[9] The Council of Europe Commissioner for Human Rights rightly points out:

> Machines function on the basis of what humans tell them. If a system is fed with human biases (conscious or unconscious) the result will inevitably be biased. The lack of diversity and inclusion in the design of AI systems is therefore a key concern: instead of making our decisions more objective, they could reinforce discrimination and prejudices by giving them an appearance of objectivity. There is increasing evidence that women, ethnic minorities, people with disabilities and LGBTQI+ persons particularly suffer from discrimination by biased algorithms.[10]

We will not present the self-regulations of the platforms here as they clearly don't work. Instead, we will examine existing binding laws. We will show the legal landscape with examples of national laws. However, since cyberviolence is a global problem that requires global solutions and siloed, national approaches cannot solve the issue,[11] we will focus on three international and regional legal systems. Two of them – the systems of the UN and the Council of Europe – are also human rights protection systems and they could be of significant importance in terms of the number of member states and possible legal impact. The third system is the EU system, which has recently developed legal developments concerning the digital area.

National frameworks

Many States do not have a holistic legal framework on combating and preventing violence against women concerning specific provisions on online and ICT-facilitated violence against women. In cases where criminal law gaps exist, victims have attempted to seek recourse through civil means, but this does not adequately address their rights to justice and remedy, contributing to continuing impunity.[12]

Legislation on cyberviolence in the EU Member States varies. European Institute for Gender Equality (EIGE) summarizing the findings on laws in 2022 indicated there's a high degree of variety, overlap, and disharmony of legal definitions of cyberviolence across Member States.[13] EIGE underlines that provisions tend to be gender neutral and no specific reference to women and girls is made in these provisions in the great majority of national legislation of Member States. EIGE indicates available definitions do not account for the complexity, gender, intersectionality, vulnerability, specific harms, the continuum of violence across digital and physical spaces of cyberviolence against women. On the other hand, the national policies (like national action plans, national strategies, and action plans) of some EU Member States mention cyberviolence against women in the context of domestic violence, and some national policies are oriented toward children and young people. Research and data collection policies vary across Member States, and different sources are used to collect data on the various forms of cyberviolence against women.[14] No Member State has specific provisions covering all forms of cyberviolence against women. In criminal laws, general offenses applying in the physical sphere (e.g. harassment and stalking) are extended to the digital sphere (e.g. cyber harassment and cyber stalking) in most Member States. In selected Member States, references to cyberviolence are made. The use of information and communication technologies is considered an aggravating circumstance in some Member States. Some Member States have adopted specific laws, including criminal code regulations to tackle certain forms of cyber violence such as cyberbullying, cyberharassment, cyberstalking, and hate speech. But not all forms of cyberviolence are criminalized.[15] The analysis commissioned by the European Parliament's Policy Department for Citizens' Rights and Constitutional Affairs confirms levels of criminalization for different forms of cyber gender-based violence vary across the EU, including whether they are criminalized directly or through aggravating circumstances. Criminalization of online forms of GBV is also very mixed, with non-consensual dissemination of private images criminalized in 16 Member States, cyber stalking criminalized in 17 Member States, cyber harassment and cyber incitement to violence or hatred criminalized in 2 and 7 Member States, respectively. Six Member States only provide online reporting options for cybercrimes (including, sometimes explicitly, online GBV). Four Member States only provide online reporting options for discrimination and/or hate crimes.[16]

An example of the EU Member State law that aims to concretize and strengthen the enforcement of significant platforms' notice and takedown obligations was the Act to Improve Enforcement of the Law in Social Networks, so-called Network Enforcement Act that was passed in 2017 in Germany (*Gesetz zur Verbesserung der Rechtsdurchsetzung in sozialen Netzwerken* so-called NetzDG). Social networks with more than 2 million registered users were required to provide effective complaints management and remove or block unlawful content under certain provisions of the German Criminal Code within a specific time frame after being notified about the content. This obligation existed with regard to content fulfilling, e.g. section 130 (incitement to hatred), section 241 (threatening the commission of a felony), section 185 (insult), section 186 (defamation), section 187 (intentional defamation), and section 201a (violation of intimate privacy by taking photographs) of the Criminal Code. In connection with this, the act also provided for the possibility of fines for social networks up to 50 million Euros for demonstrated systemic shortcomings in fulfilling compliance obligations.[17] Besides mandating platforms to promptly examine and respond to complaints (generally within 24 hours), it also required them to ensure that complaints were reviewed and handled by staff with appropriate training, German language skills and subject-matter expertise, including German law. NetzDG was criticized for its narrow focus on reactive reporting and removal of individual pieces of illegal content.[18] On the other hand, the platforms criticized the obligations adopted in the law, and the law was challenged in court.[19] Eventually, the EU Digital Service Act has replaced NetzDG in most aspects.

An example of a law on prevention and awareness-raising measures is Spanish Organic Law 10/2022 on the Comprehensive Guarantee of Sexual Freedom. The law establishes mandatory initial training for all professionals involved in dealing with sexual violence, including digital forms of sexual violence. The law requires the development of specific training programs to guarantee the specialization of professionals with direct responsibility for preventing and detecting sexual violence, as well as in comprehensive care, protection, and justice, in social services, and in law enforcement, including the Police.[20]

Other examples of legislation on cyberviolence in different areas of measures are laws adopted outside the EU, such as in the UK, Australia, and the United States.

The Online Safety Act adopted in the UK in 2023 aims to reduce online harms caused by 'user to-user', social media and 'search services' by imposing 'duties of care'.[21] The duties of care require companies to conduct risk assessments and mitigate identified risks. All in-scope services must protect all UK users from illegal content and children from certain online harms. The law includes some detailed rules concerning children since their protection was a key focus of the legislation. However, experts recommend further reforms of the law to fortify and clarify the regulatory regime, aiming to reduce the harms.[22]

In Australia there is currently no nationwide criminal statute addressing digital abuse. Of Australia's nine jurisdictions, eight have adopted legislation regarding image-based abuse.[23] There are gaps in other Australian state and territory laws where no specific criminal offenses exist.[24] However, the Australian Government established the Office of the eSafety Commissioner (till 2017 the Children's eSafety Commissioner), and in 2021, they streamlined online safety laws under the Online Safety Act. The eSafety Commissioner can investigate complaints and impose a formal warning or removal notice. The failure to comply is subject to a civil penalty of up to 500 penalty points ($ 165,000 to individual and $ 825,000 to a body corporate).[25]

In the United States, all 50 states, including the District of Columbia and U.S. territories, have stalking laws, though they vary in definition.[26] Many stalking laws can be broad enough to encompass stalking via e-mail or other electronic communication, defining the prohibited conduct in terms of 'communication', 'harassment', or 'threats' without specifying the means of such behavior, and others have specifically defined stalking via e-mail within their stalking or harassment statute.[27] However, there is legislative disparity in addressing emotional distress (recognized by Cyberbullying Research Center in 37 states) and the subjective or objective fear standard.[28] In addition, there is a federal legislation (U.S. Code § 2261A – Stalking). It makes it unlawful to travel across state lines or use the mail or computer and electronic communication services with the intent to kill, injure, harass, or intimidate another person, and as a result, place that person in reasonable fear of death or serious bodily injury or cause substantial emotional distress to that person, a spouse or intimate partner of that person, a member of that person's family or companion animal.[29] The 2022 Violence against Women Act (VAWA) reauthorization contained new provisions related to the dissemination of non-consensual pornography.[30] In addition, so-called DEFIANCE Act (Disrupt Explicit Forged Images and Non-Consensual Edits Act) of 2024 is pending deliberation by the House of Representatives. It would hold accountable those who are responsible for the proliferation of nonconsensual, sexually-explicit 'deepfake' images and videos.[31]

The United Nations and worldwide standards

The UN is the world's largest international organization. It addresses cyberviolence against women through soft law documents and binding treaties.

First, the Beijing Platform for Action, adopted in 1995 at the Fourth Conference on Women by 189 countries, is worth mentioning. It includes 'Violence against women' as one of the critical areas. While comprehensive, a global agenda for achieving gender equality is a political declaration of governments.

Second, various resolutions refer directly or indirectly to the issue of cyberviolence against women. They are political declarations, too. In its resolution 20/8 'The promotion, protection and enjoyment of human rights on the Internet' of 2012 the Human Rights Council affirms that the same rights that people have offline must also be protected online.[32] In 2013, the General Assembly, in its resolution 68/181 on protecting women human rights defenders, underlines that information-technology-related violations, abuses, discrimination, and violence against women, to discredit them and/or incite other violations and abuses against them, are a growing concern.[33] It calls upon States to exercise due diligence in preventing violations and abuses against human rights defenders, including through practical steps to prevent threats, harassment, and violence against women human rights defenders, who face particular risks, and in combating impunity by ensuring that those responsible for violations and abuses, including gender-based violence and threats against women human rights defenders, committed by State and non-State actors, including online, are promptly brought to justice through impartial investigations. In 2015, the Human Rights Council, in its resolution 29/14 on accelerating efforts to eliminate domestic violence as a form of violence against women, recognizes the latter could include acts such as cyberbullying and cyberstalking.[34] In 2016, the General Assembly, in its resolution 71/199 'The right to privacy in the digital age', calls upon States to further develop or maintain, preventive measures, and remedies for violations and abuses regarding the right to privacy in the digital age that may affect all individuals, including where there are particular effects for women.[35]

In 2018, the Human Rights Council, in its resolution 38/5 'Accelerating efforts to eliminate violence against women and girls: preventing and responding to violence against women and girls in digital contexts'[36] urges States to encourage digital technology companies to strengthen or adopt positive measures, including internal policies, to promote gender equality in the design, implementation, and use of digital technologies to eliminate violence against women and girls, and to refrain from presenting women and girls as inferior beings and exploiting them as sexual objects. States must also take immediate action to prevent all forms of violence against women by holding perpetrators to account and combating impunity for all forms of violence, including violence used to intimidate women and girls who are exercising the right to freedom of opinion and expression. The Resolution also underlines the need to encourage business enterprises in the effective implementation of the Guiding Principles on Business and Human Rights, to protect the private data of women and girls, to create transparent and effective processes for reporting violence and to develop policies that meaningfully protect women and girls from violence in digital contexts.

Human Rights Council Resolution 49/21 (2022) on 'Role of States in countering the negative impact of disinformation on the enjoyment and realization of human rights disinformation and human rights' recognizes that online disinformation campaigns are increasingly being used to deter women from participating in the public sphere, and that women journalists, women politicians, women human rights defenders, and advocates for women's rights are targeted in particular. It invites States to encourage business enterprises, including social media companies, to address disinformation while respecting human rights, including through the review of business models, in particular the role of algorithms and ranking systems in amplifying disinformation, enhancing transparency, enforcing all applicable legal protections for users, and encouraging due diligence in line with the Guiding Principles on Business and Human Rights.[37]

The recent General Assembly Resolution, 'Seizing the opportunities of safe, secure, and trustworthy artificial intelligence systems for sustainable development', was the first UN resolution on AI.[38] It emphasizes that human rights and fundamental freedoms must be respected, protected, and promoted throughout the life cycle of AI systems. It calls upon all Member States and, where applicable, other stakeholders to refrain from or cease the use of AI systems that are impossible to operate in compliance with international human rights law or that pose undue risks to the enjoyment of human rights and reaffirms that the same rights that people have offline must also be protected online. The Resolution mentions gender in only one point calling on Member States to

> adopt specific measures to close the gender digital divide and to ensure that particular attention is paid to access, affordability, digital literacy, privacy and online safety, to enhance the use of digital technologies, including artificial intelligence systems, and to mainstream a disability, gender and racial equality perspective in policy decisions and the frameworks that guide them.

The Guiding Principles on Business and Human Rights, that were mentioned in many documents, including in a few of the above, were developed by the Special Representative of the Secretary-General on the issue of human rights and transnational corporations and other business enterprises and endorsed by the Human Rights Council in its resolution 17/4 of 2011.[39] They include 31 principles on the state duty to protect human rights, the corporate responsibility to respect human rights, and access to remedy for victims of business-related abuses. States should enforce laws that are aimed at, or have the effect of, requiring business enterprises to respect human rights. The responsibility to respect human rights requires that business enterprises avoid causing or contributing to adverse human rights impacts through their activities, and address such impacts when they occur, and seek to prevent or mitigate adverse human rights impacts that are directly linked to their operations, products, or services by their business relationships, even if they have not contributed to those impacts. To identify, prevent, mitigate, and account for how they address their adverse human rights impacts, business enterprises should carry out human rights due diligence. The process should include assessing actual and potential human rights impacts, integrating and acting upon the findings, tracking responses, and communicating how impacts are addressed. Business enterprises should comply with all applicable laws and respect internationally recognized human rights, wherever they operate. While the Guiding Principles on Business and Human Rights affirm the responsibility of business enterprises to respect human rights in general, they do not make any direct reference to the Convention on the Elimination of All Forms of Discrimination against Women (CEDAW) or other women's rights instruments.[40]

Thirdly, the documents of the UN Commission on the Status of Women should be mentioned. In 2013, in Agreed Conclusions of its 57th session 'Elimination and prevention of all forms of violence against women and girls' the Commission on the Status of Women urged States to support the development and use of ICT and social media as a resource for the empowerment of women and girls, including access to information on the prevention of and response to violence against women and girls and develop mechanisms to combat the use of ICT and social media to perpetrate violence against women and girls, including the criminal misuse of ICT for sexual harassment, sexual exploitation, child pornography and trafficking in women and girls, and emerging forms of violence, such as cyberstalking, cyberbullying, and privacy violations that compromise the safety of women and girls.[41] Ten years later, the Agreed Conclusions of the 67th session of the Commission on the Status of Women concerned 'Innovation and technological change, and education in the digital age for achieving gender equality and the empowerment of all women and girls'.[42] The Commission recognized the need to address challenges associated with the misuse of new and emerging digital technologies, which can be designed and/or used to incite violence, hatred, discrimination, and hostility, and negative stereotyping and stigmatization of women and girls. The need of the zero-tolerance policy in the digital environment for all forms of violence against women and girls was underlined. The Commission urged States to develop, amend, and expand legislation and policies and strengthen their implementation by including victim- and survivor-informed responses and fast-track processes to prevent, eliminate, and respond to all forms of violence against women and girls that occur through or are amplified by the use of technology. It called on governments to ensure also private sector entities prioritize the prevention and elimination of TFGBV, including improved content moderation and curation and the interoperability, transparency, accessibility, and effectiveness of reporting systems, including by establishing robust and reliable content removal processes that would be fully compliant with relevant obligations under international human rights law.

In addition, the UN Sustainable Development Goals (SDG) concern the issue of violence against women and girls. SDG 5 on gender equality aims to 'eliminate all forms of violence against all women and girls in the public and private spheres, including trafficking and sexual and other types of exploitation' (target 5.2) and 'enhance the use of enabling technology, in particular information and communications technology, to promote the empowerment of women' (target 5.b). SDG 16 on peace, justice and strong institutions aims to 'significantly reduce all forms of violence and related death rates everywhere' (target 16.1).

A Pact for the Future should be also mentioned adopted on September 22, 2024, by world leaders at the Summit of the Future. It includes a Global Digital Compact (GDC) as 'a comprehensive framework for global governance of digital technology and artificial intelligence to harness the immense potential of digital technology and close digital divides'.[43] According to the GDC the cooperation of the Heads of State and Government should 'counter and eliminate all forms of violence, including sexual and gender-based violence that occurs through or is amplified by the use of technology'. They declare to 'establish and maintain robust risk mitigation and redress measures that also protect privacy and freedom of expression'. They also commit, by 2030, to creating a safe and secure online space for all users by defining and adopting common standards, guidelines, and industry actions that comply with international law, promote safe civic spaces, and address content on digital platforms that causes harm to individuals. In consultation with all relevant stakeholders, they want to develop effective methodologies to measure, monitor, and counter all forms of violence and abuse in the digital space.

The GDC refers to SDGs No 5, 9, 10, 16, 17, and calls on:

- digital technology companies and developers to respect international human rights and principles, including through the application of human rights due diligence and impact assessments throughout the technology life cycle;
- digital technology companies, developers, and social media platforms to respect human rights online, be accountable for and take measures to mitigate and prevent abuses, and to provide access to effective remedy in line with the United Nations Guiding Principles on Business and Human Rights and other relevant frameworks;
- digital technology companies and social media platforms to enhance the transparency and accountability of their systems, including terms of service, content moderation and recommendation algorithms, and handling of users' personal data in local languages, to empower users to make informed choices and provide or withdraw informed consent;
- social media platforms to provide researchers access to data, with safeguards for user privacy, to ensure transparency and accountability to build an evidence base on how to address misinformation and disinformation and hate speech that can inform government and industry policies, standards and best practices.

All of these documents include essential declarations, but they are not binding laws. The UN treaties, including the CEDAW, could be an important tool for combating cyberviolence against women.

The CEDAW Convention was adopted by the United Nations General Assembly in 1979.[44] It is an international legal instrument that requires countries to eliminate discrimination against women and girls in all areas. CEDAW Convention is often described as the international bill of rights for women. Almost all countries ratified it, but the United States (which only signed the Convention), Iran, Somalia, and Sudan (which have no action in the cases of both of these countries). The Convention doesn't include provisions on violence against women. It predates the development of information and communication technologies. Still, its interpretations in the form of general recommendations provided by the treaty body – the Committee on the Elimination of Discrimination against Women (the CEDAW Committee) – clearly explain how its provisions apply to the issue. In its General Recommendation No. 19 'Violence against women' of 1992 the CEDAW Committee recognizes that the definition of discrimination in Article 1 of the CEDAW Convention includes gender-based violence, that is, violence that is directed against a woman because she is a woman or that affects women disproportionately and recognized that gender-based violence may breach specific provisions of the Convention (including Articles 2, 5, 10, 16), regardless of whether those provisions expressly mention violence.[45] In 2017 the CEDAW Committee adopted General Recommendation 35 on 'Gender-based violence against women', updating General Recommendation No. 19.[46] It recognizes new forms of violence against women 'as contemporary forms of violence occurring online and in other digital environments'. The Recommendation reminds that Article 2 (e) of the Convention explicitly provides that State parties are to take all appropriate measures to eliminate discrimination against women by any person, organization or enterprise. Accordingly, States parties are to be held responsible should they fail to take all appropriate measures to prevent, as well as to investigate, prosecute, punish, and provide reparations for, acts or omissions by non-State actors that result in gender-based violence against women. It calls upon States to encourage the creation or strengthening of self-regulatory mechanisms by media organizations, including online or social media organizations, aimed at the elimination of gender stereotypes relating to women and men, or to specific groups of women, and addressing gender-based violence against women that takes place through their services and platforms.

Cyberviolence against women may violate also other binding UN human rights treaties specifying different human rights and freedoms, including the right to freedom of expression and access to information, and the right to privacy and data protection,[47] that are stated in the International Covenant on Civil and Political Rights (ICCPR) in particular.[48] First, it's the Article 19 of the ICCPR on the freedom of expression. It guarantees the right of everyone 'to hold opinions without interference' and 'to seek, receive and impart information and ideas, regardless of frontiers, either orally, in writing or print, in the form of art, or through any other media'. As the UN Special Rapporteur on the promotion of freedom of expression underlined, 'The internet should be a platform for everyone to exercise their rights to freedom of opinion and expression, but online gender-based abuse and violence assaults basic principles of equality under international law and freedom of expression'.[49] Second, cyberviolence against women in many of its forms violates the right to privacy, which is recognized under Article 17 of the ICCPR. It states that 'no one shall be subjected to arbitrary or unlawful interference with his privacy, family, home or correspondence, nor unlawful attacks on his honour and reputation' and 'everyone has the right to the protection of the law against such interference or attacks'. In its report of 2018, the Special Rapporteur on the right to privacy recognizes cyber-based violence as a contemporary obstacle to protecting and promoting the right to privacy, highlights the need to examine cyberviolence against the more vulnerable, including domestic violence enabled by digital devices, and embeds gender and other biases in algorithms.[50] The provisions of the Convention on the Rights of Persons with Disabilities adopted in 2006 should also be taken into account, including Article 21 on freedom of expression and opinion, and access to information, and Article 22 on respect for privacy.[51]

The United Nations General Assembly recently adopted the United Nations Convention against Cybercrime. According to the UN, the Convention is the first comprehensive global treaty on this subject, providing States with various measures to prevent and combat cybercrime.[52] However, the Convention does not include any regulation directed at cyberviolence against women.

Council of Europe – regional human rights organization

The Council of Europe is an international organization aimed at protecting human rights, democracy, and rule of law, representing 46 member states from Europe.[53] The most fundamental Council of Europe treaty on violence against women is the Convention on preventing and combating violence against women and domestic violence.[54] It is the first European treaty on combating violence against women and domestic violence. Its Preamble recognizes the structural nature of such violence, which is both a cause and a consequence of unequal power relations between women and men and which limits the full advancement of women. To overcome inequality, the Convention requires parties to implement gender equality policies and to empower women. The Convention sets out minimum standards to:

1 prevent violence against women;
2 protect its victims;
3 prosecute the perpetrators.

Failure to do so would make it the responsibility of the state.

Governments that agree to be bound by the Convention have to train professionals in close contact with victims; regularly run awareness-raising campaigns; take steps to include issues such as gender equality and non-violent conflict resolution in interpersonal relationships in teaching material; set up treatment programs for perpetrators of domestic violence and for sex offenders; work closely with NGOs; involve the media and the private sector in eradicating gender stereotypes and promoting mutual respect.[55] Regarding protection measures, it is essential to provide victims and witnesses with protection and support. This means police intervention and protection, as well as specialized support services such as shelters, telephone hotlines, etc. The Convention also defines and criminalizes the various forms of violence against women as well as domestic violence. State parties have to introduce several new offenses where they do not exist in national legislation. These may include psychological and physical violence, sexual violence and rape, stalking, female genital mutilation, forced marriage, forced abortion, and forced sterilization. In addition, state parties will need to ensure that culture, tradition or so-called 'honor' are not regarded as a justification for any of the conducts. State parties also have to carry out judicial proceedings in a manner that respects the rights of victims at all stages of the proceedings and that avoid secondary victimization.[56] According to Article 5(2), parties shall take the necessary legislative and other measures to exercise due diligence to prevent, investigate, punish, and provide reparation for acts of violence covered by the scope of this Convention that are perpetrated by non-State actors'.

The body of independent experts responsible for monitoring the implementation by the parties of the Council of Europe Convention on preventing and combating violence against women and domestic violence is the GREVIO. It draws up and publishes reports evaluating legislative and other measures taken by the parties to give effect to the provisions of the convention. GREVIO may also adopt general recommendations on themes and concepts of the convention.[57]

While the articles of the Convention don't explicitly refer to the violence online, the Explanatory Report to the Convention[58] underlines a few substantive criminal law provisions could be relevant:

1 Article 33 – Psychological violence:
Parties shall take the necessary legislative or other measures to ensure that the intentional conduct of seriously impairing a person's psychological integrity through coercion or threats is criminalised.

According to the Explanatory Report, the conduct 'can be done by various means and methods'.

2 Article 34 – Stalking:
Parties shall take the necessary legislative or other measures to ensure that the intentional conduct of repeatedly engaging in threatening conduct directed at another person, causing her or him to fear for her or his safety, is criminalised.
According to the Explanatory Report, this includes following the victim in the virtual world (chat rooms, social networking sites, etc.), and engaging in unwanted communication entails the pursuit of any active contact with the victim through any available means of communication, including modern communication tools and ICTs.

3 Article 40 – Sexual harassment:
Parties shall take the necessary legislative or other measures to ensure that any form of unwanted verbal, non-verbal or physical conduct of a sexual nature with the purpose or effect of violating the dignity of a person, in particular when creating an intimidating, hostile, degrading, humiliating or offensive environment, is subject to criminal or other legal sanction.

According to the Explanatory Memorandum, the type of conduct covered by this provision includes three primary forms of behavior: verbal, non-verbal, or physical conduct of a sexual nature unwanted by the victim. Verbal conduct refers to words or sounds expressed or communicated by the perpetrator, such as jokes, questions, remarks, and may be expressed orally or in writing. Non-verbal conduct, on the other hand, covers any expressions or communication on the part of the perpetrator that do not involve words or sounds.

What is more regarding transnational nature of cyberviolence Article 62 of the Convention on international cooperation stipulates that parties shall co-operate 'to the widest extent possible' for the purpose of preventing, combating, and prosecuting all forms of violence covered by the scope of the Convention; protecting and providing assistance to victims; and conducting investigations or proceedings concerning the offenses established in accordance with the Convention. The Explanatory Report underlines that parties should 'reduce, as far as possible, the obstacles to the rapid circulation of information and evidence'.

Article 17 in the Chapter III (Prevention) should also be indicated as it specifically refers to the participation of the 'information and communication technology sector':

Article 17 – Participation of the private sector and the media

1 Parties shall encourage the private sector, the information and communication technology sector and the media, with due respect for freedom of expression and their independence, to participate in the elaboration and implementation of policies and to set guidelines and selfregulatory standards to prevent violence against women and to enhance respect for their dignity.
2 Parties shall develop and promote, in co-operation with private sector actors, skills among children, parents and educators on how to deal with the information and communications environment that provides access to degrading content of a sexual or violent nature which might be harmful.

According to the Explanatory Report, paragraph 1 contains two different obligations. First, it requires Parties to the Convention to encourage the private sector, the information and communication technology sector, and the media, to participate not only in the development of local, regional, or national policies and efforts to prevent violence against women, but also to take part in their implementation. Secondly, it requires Parties to encourage the private sector, the ICT sector, and the media, to set guidelines and self-regulatory standards to enhance respect for the dignity of women and thus contribute to preventing violence against them. It is intended to encourage the ICT sector and the media to adopt self-regulatory standards to refrain from harmful gender stereotyping and spreading degrading images of women or imagery which associates violence and sex. Moreover, it means encouraging these actors to establish ethical codes of conduct for a rights-based, gender sensitive, and non-sensationalist media coverage of violence against women.

In 2016, the Council of Europe, in its publication on Article 17of the Convention[59] identified four possible actions that governments, the private sector, and the media can take together to prevent violence against women and domestic violence: enhancing the training of media professionals on issues related to gender equality and violence against women; promoting media self-regulation and regulation of discriminatory and violent content; forming partnerships to increase media coverage of gender equality and violence against women; and promoting cooperation on media literacy.

Furthermore, in 2021 GREVIO adopted its General Recommendation No. 1 on the digital dimension of violence against women.[60] It clarified that the definition of violence against women set out in Article 3a covers many forms of cyberviolence against women. Article 3 of the Istanbul Convention defines 'violence against women': as a violation of human rights and a form of discrimination against women and shall mean all acts of gender-based violence that result in or are likely to result in, physical, sexual, psychological, or economic harm or suffering to women, including threats of such acts, coercion, or arbitrary deprivation of liberty, whether occurring in public or in private life. GREVIO underlines also that the governments' obligations to take measures to combat all forms of violence against women should cover forms of cyber violence. GREVIO considers Article 5(2) on due diligence obligation to cover all expressions of violence against women, including digital expressions and violence perpetrated with the help of or through technology. Article 7 on state-wide effective, comprehensive, and coordinated set of policies that encompasses a multitude of measures and involves a variety of actors, agencies, and stakeholders requires the States to create comprehensive policies that include and specifically address cyberviolence in the area of prevention, support, and protection of victims and prosecution is of particular importance, because of the complex and multidimensional nature of the problem, according to the General Recommendation No. 1. The GREVIO underlines also that many of the forms of violence against women perpetrated through digital means come within the remit of intentional behavior, which States Parties to the Istanbul Convention are required to criminalize, including online psychological violence (Article 33), online or stalking committed in the digital sphere (Article 34), and sexual harassment online or through digital means (Article 40).

The General Recommendation No. 1 considers the following behavior online or through digital means to come under the definition of the conduct indicated in Article 40:

1 non-consensual image or video sharing;
2 non-consensual taking, producing or procuring of intimate images or videos (such as 'deepfakes');
3 exploitation, coercion and threats such as forced sexting, sexual extortion, rape threats, sexualized/gendered doxing, impersonation and outing;
4 sexualized bullying, such as circulating gossip or rumors about a victim's alleged sexual behavior, posting sexualized comments under the victim's

posts or photos, impersonating a victim and sharing sexual content, or sexually harassing others, thus impacting their reputation and/or livelihood, or 'outing' someone without their consent with the purpose of scaring, threatening, and body shaming;

5 cyberflashing that consists of sending unsolicited sexual images via dating or messaging applications, texts, or using Airdrop or Bluetooth technologies.

Sexist behavior such as sexist hate speech, which often constitutes a first step in the process toward physical violence, may also escalate to or incite overtly offensive and threatening acts, including sexual abuse or violence or rape, thus falling within the remit Article 40 of the Istanbul Convention.[61]

According to the GREVIO online and technology-facilitated stalking (Article 34) includes threats (of a sexual, economic, physical or psychological nature), damage to reputation, monitoring, and gathering of private information on the victim, identity theft, solicitation for sex, impersonating the victim, and harassing with accomplices to isolate the victim. It usually involves the tactic of surveilling or spying on the victim, on their various social media or messaging platforms, their e-mails and phone, stealing passwords or cracking or hacking their devices to access their private spaces, via the installation of spyware or geo-localization apps, or via stealing their devices. Perpetrators can also take on the other person's identity or monitor the victim via technology devices connected through the Internet of Things (IoT), such as smart home appliances. GREVIO elaborates on the digital dimension of psychological violence (Article 33). It indicates all forms of violence against women perpetrated in the digital sphere have a psychological impact and could be categorized as psychological violence exerted online and with the use of technology. The specific features of such violence against women increase the impact of the violence on victims. In addition, forms of psychological violence exerted in the context of domestic violence take radical forms when coupled with new technologies. For example, with the aid of the digital domain, this can take a new dimension where current or former partners have the victim's intimate images. Abusers can similarly misuse technology to track the whereabouts of their victims. Such forms of violence have a devastating mental and physical toll on women and girls. Moreover, individual acts of violence that are not criminalized may reach the threshold of psychological violence when combined with the mob mentality and repetition facilitated by the internet: a teasing comment may ascend to cyberbullying when made repetitively or by a large number of people. Certain groups of women, including politicians, journalists, human rights defenders, and activists, are particularly exposed to such violent acts. Similarities exist between experiences of cyberbullying and sexist hate speech, which, in addition to the consequences listed under paragraph 32, may also cause loss of resources, self-harm, or suicide and amount to psychological violence. Such acts can target every woman, in particular women who have reported incidents of gender-based violence, women who succeed in male-dominated domains (such as athletes and video game designers), women challenging traditional gender stereotypes, or women with intersectional identities who may be more exposed to violence because of their sex, gender, race, color, language, religion, political or other opinion, national or social origin, association with a national minority, property, birth, sexual orientation, gender identity, age, state of health, disability, marital status, migrant or refugee status, or other status. Young women aged from 18 to 29 years also constitute a group more at risk of violence as they are more active on the internet, including on social media. Online psychological violence can also take the form of intimidation, threatening the victims or their family, insults, shaming, and defamation. Incitement to suicide or self-harm is also a specific behavior occurring online, often amplified by the mechanisms of mob mentality and anonymity. Another form of psychological violence is economic abuse, which is defined as controlling a woman's ability to acquire, use, and maintain financial resources. Economic abuse usually occurs within the context of intimate-partner violence, and, among its negative impacts on the physical health of victims such as risk of poverty and reduced access to health care, it also threatens the victim's financial well-being and independence and consequently affects their psychological integrity seriously. In digital forums, economic abuse can manifest itself as controlling the bank accounts and financial activities of the victim through Internet banking, damaging the victim's credit rating by using credit cards without permission or filing all financial contracts (leases, loans, utilities, etc.) in the name of the victim and failing to make payments on time or at all (in particular alimony payments).[62]

As GREVIO underlines the Istanbul Convention requires States Parties to take sustained measures that aim to prevent violence against women by addressing its root causes and working to change attitudes, gender roles, and stereotypes that make violence against women acceptable. States should recognize the digital dimension of violence against women as a form of gender-based violence against women by taking the necessary legislative and other measures to promote and protect the right for everyone, particularly women, to live free from violence in both the public and the private sphere in accordance with Article 4 of the Istanbul Convention. What is more the Istanbul Convention requires States Parties to protect women and girls who are known to be at risk and to set up specialist support services for victims and their children, including shelters, round-the-clock telephone helplines, and rape crisis or sexual violence referral centers. The permanence and outreach of online content necessitate the implementation of continuous protective measures to address the digital dimension of violence against women effectively. The prevention and treatment of perpetrators of violence against women should be enhanced by gender-sensitive training on digital types of violence and the harmful stereotypes that underline them, on as well as the technological structures and features that facilitate them.[63]

The first legal instrument of the Council of Europe was the Convention for the Protection of Human Rights and Fundamental Freedoms, known as the

European Convention on Human Rights (ECHR), signed in 1950.[64] Violence against women, including cyberviolence, can violate following provisions of ECHR: Article 3 – prohibition of torture, inhuman, or degrading treatment or punishment; Article 8 – right to respect for private and family life; Article 10 – freedom of expression; Article 13 – right to an effective remedy; and Article 14 – prohibition of discrimination. The European Court of Human Rights is a judicial body that guarantees the rights enshrined in the ECHR for everyone under the jurisdiction of a State-Party of the Convention. According to Article 41 of the ECHR the Court has the power under to award 'just satisfaction' from the state to those who have suffered violations of their Convention rights that can be used to compensate for pecuniary or non-pecuniary damage, as well as for legal costs and expenses. The ECHR ruled in a few cases concerning cyberviolence against women, including the cyberviolence perpetrated by an intimate partner:

- Buturuga v. Romania, 2020[65] – the ECHR ruled that the state had violated the Convention by failing to investigate and act on cyberviolence complaints adequately;
- Volodina v. Russia, 2019[66] – the court ruled the state had failed in its positive obligation to protect victim's right to respect for private life from the acts of cyber violence she suffered, including the publication of her intimate photographs without consent, stalking, and impersonation, and that it had failed to carry out an effective investigation into these acts;
- K.U. v. Finland, 2009[67] – the ECHR ruled that the state had violated its positive obligation to protect its citizens against cybercrime, e.g. sharing pictures in an advertisement of sexual nature without consent, by identifying and prosecuting the perpetrator.

In addition, Article 10 of the ECHR protects the freedom of expression and information. It needs to be underlined in the context of online hate speech that according to the ECHR judgments states are required to create a favorable environment for participation in public debate by all the persons concerned, enabling them to 'express their opinions and ideas without fear'.[68] What is more, Article 17 of the Convention states:

> Nothing in [the] Convention may be interpreted as implying for any State, group or person any right to engage in any activity or perform any act aimed at the destruction of any of the rights and freedoms set forth herein or at their limitation to a greater extent than is provided for in the Convention.

Some forms of expression are not protected by the right to free expression. The freedom of expression guaranteed under Article 10 of the Convention may not be invoked in a sense contrary to Article 17, and Article 10 does not cover certain forms of hate speech.[69] In the case Delfi AS v. Estonia, 2015,[70] the ECHR didn't find a violation of Article 10 and the rights of a news portal ruling it was proportionate to hold it liable for hosting hateful comments – even though it had not known about them and on being notified had removed them. The court took into account the extreme nature of the comments, the fact that the comments were posted in reaction to an article published on professionally managed news portal run on a commercial basis, the insufficiency of the measures taken by the portal to remove without delay after publication comments amounting to hate speech and speech inciting violence and to ensure a realistic prospect of the authors of such comments being held liable. The court finds that the domestic courts' imposition of liability on the applicant company was based on relevant and sufficient grounds. Therefore, the measure did not constitute a disproportionate restriction on the applicant company's right to freedom of expression.

The Convention on Cybercrime of the Council of Europe, so-called Budapest Convention, adopted in 2001, could be supplementary in prosecution of cyberviolence as it is regarded as the most comprehensive and coherent international agreement on cybercrime and electronic evidence to date.[71] It requires its parties to criminalize conducts perpetrated against or by means of computer data and systems, ranging from illegal access, data, and systems interference to computer-related fraud and child pornography. It provides procedural powers to investigate cybercrime and secure electronic evidence in relation to any crime, as well as for efficient international cooperation. The First Additional Protocol to the Convention on Cybercrime of 2003 concerns the criminalization of acts of a racist and xenophobic nature committed through computer systems. This Protocol entails an extension of the Cybercrime Convention's scope, including its substantive, procedural, and international cooperation provisions, to cover also offenses of racist or xenophobic propaganda. Thus, apart from harmonizing the substantive law elements of such behavior, the Protocol aims to improve the Parties' ability to use the means and avenues of international cooperation set out in the Convention in this area.[72] The treaty body is the Cybercrime Convention Committee, which ensures the effective implementation of the Convention. The analyses show that the framework of cybercrime (the Budapest Convention) can be applied to the phenomenon of online and technology-facilitated violence against women (the Istanbul Convention) to some extent,[73] including substantive and procedural provisions and articles on international cooperation.

The Cybercrime Convention Committee indicates two of the substantive provisions of the Budapest Convention that have a direct connection to cyberviolence and others that could cover conduct that may facilitate such violence. The procedural tools and international cooperation tools would apply in any case.[74] Two articles of the substantive criminalization section of the Budapest Convention that could be utilized in connection with cyberviolence against women are Article 4 – Data interference and Article 5 – System interference. Other substantive articles criminalize acts that could be involved in cyberviolence:

- Article 2 – illegal access to a victim's system is common in cyberthreats, cyberstalking, sextortion, and other forms of privacy violations amounting to cyberviolence. A third party's system may be accessed illegally to be used as a platform for messages or attacks or the theft of intimate data.
- Article 3 – illegal interception – incoming or outgoing traffic may be illegally intercepted to hinder communication with law enforcement or show a victim that the attacker knows everything the victim does. Traffic may also be intercepted to commit privacy violations amounting to cyberviolence, such as image-based sexual abuse.
- Article 6 – misuse of devices. A criminal may harvest passwords from a target system – a school, an organization, etc. – to use its internal system to transmit threats.
- Article 7 – computer-related forgery may be used to fake authorization to enter a building.
- Article 11 – attempting, aiding, and abetting some or all of the crimes in Articles 2–10.

As far as procedural law of the Budapest Convention is concerned Article 14 provides that countries must apply the Budapest Convention's procedural law provisions to the substantive offenses in the Convention, to other criminal offenses committed by means of a computer system, and to the collection of evidence in electronic form of any criminal offense. The procedural tools thus are available to pursue cyberviolence in any form. Those tools include expedited preservation of stored computer data (Article 16); expedited preservation and partial disclosure of traffic data (Article 17); production orders (Article 18); search and seizure of stored computer data (Article 19); real-time collection of traffic data (Article 20); interception of content data (Article 21). The Articles 16 to 21 of the Budapest Convention could supplement the Istanbul Convention in the context of prosecuting cyberviolence against women. Regarding international cooperation, Article 23 requires Parties to cooperate to the greatest extent possible under any relevant instrument or law, 'for the purposes of investigations or proceedings concerning criminal offences related to computer systems and data, or for the collection of evidence in electronic form of a criminal offence'. The international cooperation provisions of the Budapest Convention include: extradition (Article 24); general principles on mutual assistance (Article 25); spontaneous information (Article 26); mutual assistance in the absence of international agreements (Article 27); confidentiality and use limitations (Article 28); expedited preservation of stored computer data (Article 29); expedited disclosure of preserved traffic data (Article 30); mutual assistance in accessing of stored computer data (Article 31); trans-border access to stored computer data with consent or where publicly available (Article 32); mutual assistance in the real-time collection of traffic data (Article 33); mutual assistance in the interception of content data (Article 34).

The Cybercrime Convention Committee points out the Budapest and Istanbul Conventions appear to be complementary with regard to substantive criminal law. A country implementing the Budapest Convention should thus consider also implementation of Articles 33, 34, and 40 of the Istanbul Convention to combat psychological violence, stalking, and sexual harassment in an online context. Conversely, the Istanbul Convention does not include specific provisions to secure electronic evidence in domestic and international investigations related to online violence against women. Countries implementing the Istanbul Convention should thus consider implementing the procedural powers of Articles 16 to 21 of the Budapest Convention and facilitating international cooperation on electronic evidence (Articles 23–35 of the Budapest Convention) in relation to online violence against women.[75]

The Council of Europe addresses cyberviolence against women through its various soft-law instruments, including recommendations and resolutions:

1 Recommendation CM/Rec(2014)6 of the Committee of Ministers to member States on a Guide to human rights for Internet users[76] – the Committee of Ministers underlines the corporate social responsibility of online service providers includes a commitment to combating hate speech and other content that incites violence or discrimination. Online service providers should be attentive to the use of, and editorial responses to, expressions motivated by racist, xenophobic, anti-Semitic, misogynist, sexist (including as regards LGBTQI+ people), or other bias. These providers should also be ready to help Internet users report content or expression of views and/or behavior that may be considered illegal.
2 Resolution 2144 (2017) of the Parliamentary Assembly 'Ending cyberdiscrimination and online hate'[77] concerns the diverse grounds on which people are today targeted by hate speech and taking into account the rapidly evolving forms of online hate and of the media through which it is disseminated.
3 Recommendation CM/Rec(2018)2 of the Committee of Ministers to member States on the roles and responsibilities of Internet intermediaries[78] indicates responsibilities of Internet intermediaries with respect to human rights and fundamental freedoms that States should aim to ensure. The responsibility of intermediaries to respect human rights and to employ adequate measures applies regardless of their size, sector, operational context, ownership structure, or nature. The more significant the impact and the potential damage to the objects of legal protection and the higher the value of the services for the exercise of human rights, the greater the precautions that the intermediary should employ when developing and applying their terms and conditions of service, community standards, and codes of ethics aiming, notably, to prevent the spread of abusive language and imagery, of hatred and incitement to violence.

4 Recommendation CM/Rec(2019)1 of the Committee of Ministers to Member States on preventing and combating sexism.[79] This text contains the first ever internationally agreed definition of sexism, which is:

> 'Any act, gesture, visual representation, spoken or written words, practice or behavior based upon the idea that a person or a group of persons is inferior because of their sex, which occurs in the public or private sphere, whether online or offline, with the purpose or effect of:
>
> i violating the inherent dignity or rights of a person or a group of persons; or
> ii resulting in physical, sexual, psychological or socio-economic harm or suffering to a person or a group of persons; or
> iii creating an intimidating, hostile, degrading, humiliating or offensive environment; or
> iv constituting a barrier to the autonomy and full realization of human rights by a person or a group of persons; or
> v maintaining and reinforcing gender stereotypes'.

The recommendation proposes specific tools and measures to prevent and combat sexism and sexist behavior in language and communications, the Internet and social media, and media and advertising. It indicates that sexism and sexist behavior occur across the full range of human activity, including cyberspace (the Internet and social media). The Internet has provided a new dimension for the expression and transmission of sexism, especially sexist hate speech, to a large audience.

5 Recommendation CM/Rec(2022)16 of the Committee of Ministers to Member States in combating hate speech[80] includes the measure on the legislation regarding online hate speech. Member States should ensure that their legislation addressing hate speech covers offline as well as online hate speech and contains clear and foreseeable provisions for the swift and effective removal of online hate speech that is prohibited under criminal, civil, or administrative law. Removal procedures and conditions and related responsibilities and liability rules imposed on Internet intermediaries should be transparent, clear, and predictable, and those procedures should be subject to due process. The duties include rapid processing of reports of such hate speech; removing such hate speech without delay; respecting privacy and data protection requirements; securing evidence relating to hate speech prohibited under criminal law; reporting cases of such criminal hate speech to the authorities; transmitting to the law-enforcement services, based on an order issued by the competent authority, evidence relating to criminal hate speech; referring unclear and complex cases requiring further assessment to competent self-regulatory or co-regulatory institutions or authorities; and foreseeing the possibility of implementing, in unclear and complex cases, provisional measures such as deprioritization or contextualization.

6 The Council of Europe's Gender Equality Strategy 2024–2029 underlines that examples of platforms that act as conveyers of sexism and sexist hate speech include social media, pornography, and video games. Freedom of expression is often abused as the pretext to avoid accountability for unacceptable and offensive behavior. In the same way as with other forms of violence against women and girls, sexist hate speech remains underreported. Still, its impact, especially on girls and young women, be it emotional, psychological, and/or physical, is devastating. Technology-facilitated violence is a growing global problem which affects women and girls disproportionately. The digital dimension of violence against women and girls manifests itself as part of a continuum of violence, which is connected to violence offline. It represents yet another form of abuse and silencing embedded within existing gender-based power structures. Violent acts that rely on and are facilitated by technology are an integral part of the same violence that women and girls experience in the offline world based on their sex and intersecting identities. Violence and abuse online can limit women's right to express themselves equally, freely, and without fear, including in political and public life.

Work is currently underway within the Council of Europe to address technology-facilitated violence against women and girls. The Committee of Experts on Combating Technology-Facilitated Violence against Women and Girls, established as a joint subcommittee of the Gender Equality Commission and the European Committee on Crime Problems, has been mandated by the Committee of Ministers to draft its Recommendation by 2025. The forthcoming instrument is expected to build on existing standards, including GREVIO's General Recommendation No. 1 on the digital dimension of violence against women, and to provide guidance for Member States in ensuring effective legal remedies, particularly in criminal law, as well as in developing comprehensive policy approaches to prevent and combat such forms of violence.[81]

The European Union and its recent development on the digital sphere

The EU is a political and economic union of 27 member states located primarily in Europe. At the EU level, several pieces of legislation, including regulations and directives, or soft law as European Parliament resolutions and European Commission policies, could apply to various forms of cyberviolence against women. Specific EU instruments, such as the General Data Protection Regulation (GDPR), the Digital Services Act (DSA), the Regulation on e-Evidence, the Artificial Intelligence Act, or the Victims' Rights Directive and the Audiovisual Media Services Directive are legally binding for Member States, whereas other instruments, such as the Code of Conduct on Countering Illegal Hate Speech Online is considered self-regulation but could be usefully to some degree.[82]

Regulation (EU) 2016/679 of the European Parliament and of the Council of April 27, 2016, on the protection of natural persons about the processing of personal data and the free movement of such data (GDPR)[83] obliges companies that process data to request explicit consent from the user – individual.[84] GDPR does not mention any form of cyberviolence against women but violence online in the form of image-based sexual abuse could fall under the GDPR provision on 'processing of personal data' as unconsented content. The individual responsible for uploading image-based sexual abuse material as well as the publisher of such material could be considered joint data controllers (an entities that collects data from EU residents) and hence fall under the obligations and sanctions imposed by the GDPR. The regulation applies if the data controller, the processor (an organization that processes data on behalf of a data controller like cloud service providers) or the data subject (individual) is based in the EU. In this case the GDPR also contains a 'right to erasure', so-called the right to be forgotten for data subjects who no longer want their data to be processed to request that it is permanently deleted, if there are no legitimate grounds for retaining. The GDPR hasn't been used as an efficient tool to protect women from image-based sexual abuse yet.

Regulation (EU) 2022/2065 of the European Parliament and of the Council of October 19, 2022, on a Single Market for Digital Services and amending Directive 2000/31/EC (DSA)[85] aims to set out harmonized rules for a safe, predictable, and trusted online environment that facilitates innovation and in which fundamental rights enshrined in the Charter, including the principle of consumer protection, are effectively protected. It maintains the liability regime inherited from the Directive on e-Commerce, in which platforms are not liable for hosting illegal information, on condition that they either do not know about the illegal content or remove it promptly on becoming aware. The DSA establishes a set of due diligence obligations for all providers of intermediary services, hosting services, and online platforms. Generally, social media platforms fall into all three of these categories, so must comply with all these obligations.

'Illegal content' is defined in Article 3(h) DSA as any content either in itself or in relation to an activity, which is not in compliance with Union law or the law of any Member State. Illustrative examples include the unlawful non-consensual sharing of private images (Recital 12 of the Preamble). The Regulation authorizes national judicial and administrative authorities to order intermediaries to remove illegal content. The DSA requires platforms to publish their contractual content policies 'in clear, plain, intelligible, user-friendly, and unambiguous language' and to publish yearly transparency reports on content moderation. Article 16 requires platforms to implement easily accessible, user-friendly reporting systems and promptly review reported content. Article 16 requires hosting providers to operate a notice-and-action system where users can report content as illegal or incompatible with the platform's policies. Article 17 requires them to 'provide a clear and specific statement of reasons' to users whose content is restricted. Article 20 further requires platforms to establish an internal complaint handling system in which users whose content is removed, or who have reported content, which was not removed, can appeal the decision. Platforms must review complaints 'in a timely, non-discriminatory, diligent and non-arbitrary manner' and not solely automatically. Article 21 additionally empowers users to further appeal such decisions to certified out-of-court dispute settlement institutions. The DSA creates further obligations for providers of 'very large online platforms' (defined as platforms whose number of average monthly active recipients of the service in the EU equal to or higher than 45 million) to conduct regular risk assessments and take measures to mitigate various systemic risks. Article 34 provides that these risks include inter alia any actual or foreseeable negative effects in relation to gender-based violence. The platforms have already introduced a lot of these elements as a part of their internal regulations, and they have failed to protect women from cyberviolence. Hence, the question on how the DSA could change it could be raised.

Regulation (EU) 2023/1543 of the European Parliament and of the Council of July 12, 2023, on European Production Orders and European Preservation Orders for electronic evidence in criminal proceedings and the execution of custodial sentences following criminal proceedings, so-called Regulation on e-Evidence,[86] was adopted since, according to the European Commission, 'more than half of all criminal investigations today include a cross-border request to access electronic evidence such as texts, e-mails or messaging apps' to identify a perpetrator such as their IP address. This regulation allows law-enforcement agencies from any EU member state to access electronic information more rapidly by requesting it directly or requesting its preservation from online service providers in other EU countries and service providers are obliged to respond within 10 days. However it remains unclear whether service providers fully respect their obligations.

Regulation (EU) 2024/1689 of the European Parliament and of the Council of June 13, 2024, laying down harmonized rules on AI and amending Regulations (EC) No 300/2008, (EU) No 167/2013, (EU) No 168/2013, (EU) 2018/858, (EU) 2018/1139 and (EU) 2019/2144 and Directives 2014/90/EU, (EU) 2016/797, and (EU) 2020/1828 (Artificial Intelligence Act)[87] could be another essential law that addresses the problem of cyberviolence against women. Research shows that AI systems could and are used to create or manipulate materials, including intimate images or videos, without a person's consent. The goal of the Regulation could suggest the law recognizes the problem. According to Article 1 the purpose of the Regulation is to improve the functioning of the internal market and promote the uptake of human-centric and trustworthy AI, while ensuring a high level of protection of health, safety, and fundamental rights enshrined in the Charter, including democracy, the rule of law and environmental protection, against the harmful effects of AI systems in the Union and supporting innovation. However, the Regulation doesn't address the issue of cyberviolence against women. It only includes a few provisions, contained both in the preamble and in its articulated text, that refer to 'equality', 'gender equality', or 'women's equality' or, more generally, to the fundamental rights these values belong to. Moreover, while it requires deployers of an AI system that generates or manipulates image, audio, or video content constituting a deepfake, to disclose that the content has been artificially generated or manipulated, it even limits the transparency obligations where the content forms part of an evidently artistic, creative, satirical, fictional, or analogous work or program. The deployers are only obliged to disclosure of the existence of such generated or manipulated content in an appropriate manner that does not hamper the display or enjoyment of the work. The Preamble of the Regulation further explains that compliance with this transparency obligation should not be interpreted as indicating that the use of the AI system or its output impedes the right to freedom of expression and the right to freedom of the arts and sciences guaranteed in the Charter, in particular where the content is part of an evidently creative, satirical, artistic, fictional, or analogous work or program (Recital 134 of the Preamble). The Regulation doesn't recognize the threats and harms of the creation of sexually explicit deepfakes when the labeling of such content as deepfake doesn't limit the harm to the victim. Furthermore it justifies the creation of image-sexual abusive deepfakes by freedoms of the perpetrators of cyberviolence.

Directive 2012/29/EU of the European Parliament and of the Council of October 25, 2012, establishing minimum standards on the rights, support, and protection of victims of crime, and replacing Council Framework Decision 2001/220/JHA so-called Victims' Rights Directive[88] aims to ensure that persons who have fallen victim to crime are recognized and treated with respect, particularly are well informed of their rights, know where they can seek protection, can participate in criminal proceedings, and are protected both while the police investigates the crime and during court proceedings that law enforcement and the justice sector is trained to support victims. The directive protects victims of crime as defined under national laws. It is therefore applicable to forms of cyberviolence against women if they are criminalized in a given Member State. Directive makes specific reference to victims of gender-based violence, victims of sexual violence, and victims of violence in a close relationship, but mostly in its preamble. The EIGE report analyzing the Victims' Rights Directive from a gender perspective points at gaps in the provisions covering issues of support and protection for victims of gender-based violence.[89] According to EIGE, these provisions

> do not account for the specific nature of gender-based violence at all, being too general, or do not provide reference to instruments such as codes of conduct, in the absence of which, the application of legal solutions can prove limited.

Evaluation of the European Commission of the Victims' Rights Directive found in 2022 identified shortcomings in relation to victims' access to information, victims' access to support services, and protection in accordance with each victim's individual needs.[90] In the context of online harm, the evaluation found that 'the Directive is silent on digitally enabled offences such as online harassment' and that 'Stakeholders' consultations indicate that there is room for improvement in relation to the role that both the digital space and the use of communication technology could play'. The evaluation concludes, in the context of the applicability of the Directive to online conduct, that it 'may also not adequately address the needs of victims of online crime or crime enabled by new technology'.

Directive (EU) 2018/1808 of the European Parliament and of the Council of November 14, 2018, amending Directive 2010/13/EU on the coordination of specific provisions laid down by law, regulation, or administrative action in Member States concerning the provision of audiovisual media services (Audiovisual Media Services Directive)[91] in view of changing market realities applies to TV, video-on-demand services, and video-sharing platforms, including social media essentially devoted to video-sharing such as video-centric platforms like YouTube and TikTok, but also the platforms which have a dissociable section dedicated to user-generated videos, particularly Instagram's Instagram Video and Reels and Facebook's Watch section. The directive aims at protecting minors from content 'which may impair their physical, mental or moral development' and all users from content 'containing incitement to violence or hatred directed against a group of persons or a member of such a group defined by reference to sex, race, color, religion, descent or national or ethnic origin'. It also contains provisions allowing users to report harmful content for removal. Again, the Directive seems not to be an efficient tool to protect women from cyberviolence.

The Parliament has adopted numerous resolutions on issues relevant to cyberviolence against women, such as the 2020 resolution on strengthening media freedom: the protection of journalists in Europe, hate speech, disinformation, and the role of platforms;[92] the 2021 resolution with recommendations to the Commission on identifying gender-based violence as a new area of crime listed in Article 83(1) Treaty on the Functioning of the European Union (TFEU);[93] and resolution of December 14, 2021, with recommendations to the Commission on combating gender-based violence: cyberviolence.[94] The latter one recommended that the European Commission should use its forthcoming proposal for a directive on combating gender-based violence to criminalize gender-based cyber-violence, as a cornerstone for the harmonization of existing and future legal acts.

The European Commission has adopted the Gender Equality Strategy 2020–2025[95] and the Strategy on Victims' Rights 2020–2025.[96] The EU Gender

Equality Strategy acknowledges online and technology-facilitated violence against women as follows:

> Online violence targeting women has become pervasive with specific, vicious consequences; this is unacceptable. It is a barrier to women's participation in public life. Bullying, harassment and abuse on social media have far-reaching effects on women's and girls' daily lives

The EU Strategy on Victims' Rights defines cybercrime as 'any type of a criminal offence that is committed online or with a use of computer or online tools'. Furthermore, it adds: 'Victims of cybercrime do not always find relevant assistance to remedy the damage they suffered and often fail to report a crime'.

Another soft law measure is the EU Code of Conduct on Countering Illegal Hate Speech Online.[97] It was signed on May 31, 2016, by the European Commission and Google (YouTube), Facebook, Twitter, and Microsoft hosted consumer services ('the IT Companies'). In 2018 and 2019, Instagram, Google+, Dailymotion, Snap, and Jeuxvideo.com have joined. This means the Code has covered 96% of the EU market share of online platforms that may be affected by hateful content. IT Companies declare in the Code they 'share the European Commission's and EU Member States' commitment to tackle illegal hate speech online'. Illegal hate speech is defined in the Code by the Framework Decision 2008/913/JHA of November 28, 2008, on combating certain forms and expressions of racism and xenophobia by means of criminal law and national laws transposing it. It means all conduct publicly inciting to violence or hatred directed against a group of persons or a member of such a group defined by reference to race, color, religion, descent or national or ethnic origin. This way the code of conduct focuses on racist hate speech and does not explicitly tackle gender-based hate speech. The IT Companies and the European Commission also 'stress the need to defend the right to freedom of expression'. There are the following public commitments of IT Companies in the Code:

- to have in place clear and effective processes to review notifications regarding illegal hate speech on their services so they can remove or disable access to such content;
- upon receipt of a valid removal notification – to review such requests with dedicated teams reviewing requests;
- to review the majority of valid notifications for removal of illegal hate speech in less than 24 hours and remove or disable access to such content, if necessary;
- to educate and raise awareness with their users about the types of content not permitted under their rules and community guidelines;
- to provide regular training to their staff on the current societal developments and to exchange views on the potential for further improvement;

- to intensify cooperation between themselves and other platforms and social media companies to enhance best practice sharing.

As experts rightly underline, the major flaw of the monitoring activity is the lack of data disaggregation and the lack of overall transparency on reports and removals. Intersectional attacks are not accounted for, making it complicated to fully understand the phenomenon of hate speech online that contains a strong intersectional dimension and thus trivializing the experience of many women users.[98] In addition, it is unclear the extent to which data represents genuine improvements in the removal rate for illegal hate speech while Internet platforms are being aware of monitoring periods. Thirdly, organizations participating as trusted flaggers in the monitoring training sessions and meetings are being offered 'advertising grants' by Internet platforms, which raises questions about the independence, neutrality, and transparency.[99]

The seventh evaluation on the Code of Conduct on Countering Illegal Hate Speech Online shows that the number of notifications reviewed within 24 hours (64.4%) has decreased as compared to 2021 (81%) and 2020 (90.4%).[100] The average removal rate (63.6%) is similar to 2021 (62.5%), but still lower than in 2020 (71%). Looking at the individual performance of the platforms, most of them (except for YouTube) have removed less hate speech content than in 2021. Removal rates varied depending on the severity of hateful content. On average, 69.6% of content calling for murder or violence against specific groups was removed, while content using defamatory words or pictures to name certain groups, was removed in 59.1% of the cases. To date, the Code only involves voluntary commitments. However, under Article 45 DSA, such industry code can now have an official status. This means it will factor into evaluations of very large online platforms' compliance with their risk mitigation obligations under Article 35, giving them a quasi-binding character.

The most essential EU binding law on counteracting cyberviolence against women is the Directive 2024/1385 of the European Parliament and of the Council of May 14, 2024, on combating violence against women and domestic violence. Since it could have been a crucial instrument to combat cyberviolence against women at the European level, we will pay particular attention to its regulations.

The Commission proposed new legislation on combating violence against women and domestic violence, which was adopted on May 7, 2024 (Directive (EU) 2024/1385). The EU now has the first ever law to fight violence against women and domestic violence effectively. The Directive requires Member States to put in place measures of prevention, protection, access to justice, support, coordination, and cooperation between authorities. The Directive criminalizes at EU level certain forms of violence against women offline (female genital mutilation and forced marriage) and online (non-consensual sharing of intimate images, cyber stalking, cyber harassment, and incitement to hatred and violence on the ground of gender).

Article 5 of the Directive concerns non-consensual sharing of intimate or manipulated material:

1 Member States shall ensure that the following intentional conduct is punishable as a criminal offence:

   a making accessible to the public, by means of information and communication technologies ('ICT'), images, videos or similar material depicting sexually explicit activities or the intimate parts of a person, without that person's consent, where such conduct is likely to cause serious harm to that person;
   b producing, manipulating, or altering and subsequently making accessible to the public, by means of ICT, images, videos, or similar material making it appear as though a person is engaged in sexually explicit activities, without that person's consent, where such conduct is likely to cause serious harm to that person;
   c threatening to engage in the conduct referred to in point (a) or (b) in order to coerce a person to do, acquiesce to or refrain from a certain act.

2 Paragraph 1, points (a) and (b), of this Article does not affect the obligation to respect the rights, freedoms and principles referred to in Article 6 Treaty on European Union (TEU) and applies without prejudice to fundamental principles related to the freedom of expression and information and the freedom of the arts and sciences, as implemented in Union or national law.

The content of Article 5 of the Directive poses several significant risks to the effective prosecution of cyberviolence against women and access to justice for victims.

First, the phrase 'making accessible to the public' in Article 5(1) may introduce an unnecessary restriction and exclude many harmful behaviors from prosecution. As the experts rightly point out, Article 5 will certainly cover behavior involving the sharing of materials on publicly accessible websites, or forums, such as the X platform, while it raises questions of interpretation in cases of more limited distribution[101] or the case of closed groups and forums.[102] Moreover, the fact that the perpetrator will share the materials with the victim's family, friends, employer, or associates, which may not meet the criterion of public sharing, will not necessarily result in less harm to the victim. In some communities, such as some minority religious communities, disclosing information to a small number of people, while not public, may have devastating impacts, perhaps more than where images are shared with thousands of 'friends' online who are not so concerned about the intimate activity being disclosed.[103] The European Economic and Social Committee expressed similar concerns in its opinion on the proposal for a Directive, stressing that 'the reputational harm is sometimes greater if the material is shared only with people from the victim's close social, family or work circles'.[104] Thus, using the phrase 'public' Article 5 may not cover harmful sharing of intimate materials with a limited number of people, significantly reducing the effectiveness of prosecuting such behaviors.

Secondly, Article 5(1)(b) raises significant concerns – by limiting it only to manipulated content material 'making it appear as though a person is engaged in sexually explicit activities'. This expression seems to exclude, for example, the production of recordings showing situations involving the nudity of the persons in question, when such a person is not engaged in sexually explicit activities and is likely to exclude all material produced through 'nudification' apps, and subsequently distributed without consent.[105] A broader formulation referring to – in general – activities of a sexual nature and intimate body parts would be consistent with the content of Article 5(1)(a). Moreover, for the same reasons, within the scope of Article 5(1)(a), it would be necessary to criminalize behavior concerning the depiction not only of sexually explicit activities or intimate parts of a person's body without his or her consent, but also of a person's nudity without his or her consent. It is unclear whether Article 5(1)(a) and (b) include the materials produced using AI systems and non-visual content – i.e. texts or audios, the latter as mentioned in Recital 19 of the Directive's preamble.[106]

Third, Article 5(1)(c) covers only cases of threats conducted with a clearly defined motive, i.e. 'to coerce a person to do, acquiesce to or refrain from a certain act'. Indeed, this provision covers cases of blackmail, but it leaves out of its scope behavior whose purpose will be simply to cause suffering to the victim, rather than to force the victim to behave in a certain way. The reasons for the threats may also not be obvious and unambiguous, which will result in threatening to make sexual material available to the public without consent or to produce manipulated material when the aforementioned is not demonstrated will go unpunished.

Fourth, Article 5(1) contains an additional requirement to indicate the result of the behavior, i.e. 'where such conduct is likely to cause serious harm to that person'. The public sharing by means of information and communication technologies of material depicting sexually explicit activities or intimate parts of a person's body without that person's consent, or the sharing of similar material specifically produced or manipulated for this purpose, constitute in themselves sufficiently harmful behavior that violates the dignity, privacy, and other human rights of the victim. The Directive's preamble, according to which 'when assessing whether an act is likely to cause serious harm, the focus should be on whether the act would typically cause harm to a victim' (Recital 22), only confirms the risk of interpretative difficulties at the prosecution and sentencing stages and, in general, the lack of consideration of the specific nature of such behavior. The premise of the likelihood of serious harm to the victim will only create barriers to the effective prosecution of perpetrators of violence against women in cyberspace. Although serious harm can, and most often does, result from cyberviolence, its occurrence is not always clear-cut, which may prevent or limit the effectiveness of law enforcement in cases where the victim does not experience immediate consequences or finds it difficult to demonstrate or prove them.

Finally, fifth, the reference in Article 5(2) to the rights, freedoms and principles referred to in Article 6 TEU and to fundamental principles related to the freedom of expression and information and the freedom of the arts and sciences, as implemented in Union or national law, as justifying the publication of intimate material – real or manipulated – without a person's consent is seriously concerning. Significant objections and misunderstanding are raised by the statements in the Directive's preamble, according to which

> the dissemination of images, videos, or other material depicting sexually explicit activities or the intimate parts of a person without that person's consent to the public by means of ICT should not be criminalised, where such non-criminalisation is necessary to safeguard the fundamental rights protected under the Charter, in particular the freedom of expression, including the freedom to receive and impart information and ideas in an open and democratic society, as well as the freedom of the arts and sciences, including academic freedom.
>
> (Recital 20)

The freedom of expression or the freedom of the arts and sciences referred to in the preamble cannot in any way justify sexual violence and preclude the prosecution of perpetrators of such violence and the protection of its victims. Perpetrators may use this provision to explain that the nature of their activity has an artistic dimension, for example, and as such is not subject to prosecution. The purpose of the regulation is to protect victims and effectively respond to violations of their fundamental human rights, which are violated by cyberviolence, including through the public dissemination of intimate material without that person's consent. Legitimizing such behavior with, for example, artistic freedom cannot be considered right.

Article 6, the Directive's second provision on the criminalization of cyberviolence against women, implies the criminalization of cyberstalking, i.e. the intentional conduct of repeatedly or continuously placing a person under surveillance, without that person's consent or a legal authorization to do so, by means of ICT, to track or monitor that person's movements and activities, where such conduct is likely to cause serious harm to that person. In the case of this provision, the EU legislator also points to the premise of likelihood of serious harm. The considerations regarding this premise in relation to Article 5 of the Directive remain valid. In addition, the premise of 'repeated or continuous surveillance' in Article 6 is worrying, excluding the prosecution of acts if they do not meet the criterion of repetition or continuity. Cyberstalking is often accompanied by single but equally dangerous acts that can be difficult to qualify according to the literal wording of Article 6, particularly in view of the 'continuity' requirement, which is difficult to interpret. Finally, it seems unjustified to limit the prosecution of the conducts defined in Article 6 of the Directive only to those whose purpose can be clearly defined as tracking or monitoring a person's movements and activities. Cyberstalking may also be carried out for other purposes, including simply to harm the victim, cause stress, fear, anxiety, or distress to the victim, or these purposes may not be unambiguous. Their determination may raise difficulties, which will limit, and in some cases completely preclude, adequate protection of victims.

Article 7 of the Directive prohibits cyberharassment:
Member States shall ensure that the following intentional conduct is punishable as a criminal offence:

a repeatedly or continuously engaging in threatening conduct directed at a person, at least where such conduct involves threats to commit criminal offences, by means of ICT, where such conduct is likely to cause that person to seriously fear for their own safety or the safety of dependants;
b engaging, together with other persons, by means of ICT, in publicly accessible threatening or insulting conduct directed at a person, where such conduct is likely to cause serious psychological harm to that person;
c the unsolicited sending, by means of ICT, of an image, video or other similar material depicting genitals to a person, where such conduct is likely to cause serious psychological harm to that person;
d making accessible to the public, by means of ICT, material containing the personal data of a person, without that person's consent, for the purpose of inciting other persons to cause physical or serious psychological harm to that person.

Article 7 of the Directive allows for prosecution only 'repeated or continuous threat'. The concerns in this regard, cited with regard to the Article 6 of the Directive, remain valid. In addition, it criminalizes conducts that involve threats to commit criminal offenses. Cyberviolence against women involving threats against the victim will not always constitute threatening of committing criminal offenses, but other behaviors that could not be included in criminal codes. It is crucial that other harmful behaviors of perpetrators of online violence, including those that do not constitute punishable threats, do not go unpunished. The phrase 'where such conduct is likely to cause that person to seriously fear for their own safety or the safety of dependants' in Article 7(a) of the Directive, is also concerning. As several studies have shown, cyberviolence often causes victim's fear for his or her safety or that of his or her dependents. However, this depends on several factors that should not affect the impunity of the perpetrator, if the fear cannot be proved.

It should also be emphasized that the 'dependents' rationale narrows the possibility of prosecuting behavior that would cause victims to fear for the safety of, for example, their parents, spouse or partner, or adult children, in cases where these persons are not dependents. As such, it appears unnecessarily restrictive of victim protection. In addition, interpretive difficulties may be raised by the question of the 'seriousness' of the fear, and the need to resolve whether the victim is 'seriously' afraid or whether this fear is not serious significantly reduces the effectiveness of this provision. The premise 'together with other persons' in Article 7(b) of the Directive is difficult to interpret, too. Directing threats and insults should be sufficient to fulfill the elements of the offense, especially since, in this case, the prosecution is limited to conduct undertaken in public. Limiting such behavior to a situation in which the perpetrator acts together with other persons, rather than alone or individually, raises difficulties of interpretation. It is not clear what exactly is meant by directing threats and insults 'together with other persons' including – whether the perpetrator is to undertake these behaviors in an organized manner with other persons to fulfill the elements of the crime, which in the case of social media would be difficult to determine. In the case of Articles 7(b) and 7(c) of the Directive, the premise 'when such acts are likely to cause serious mental harm to that person' as the elements of the offense is troublesome. The arguments cited above remain valid here. In addition, the prosecution of acts under Article 7(c) of the Directive (cyberflashing) should not be limited to conduct involving the transmission of an image, video, or other similar content depicting genitalia, but should also cover acts involving the transmission of an image, video or other similar content also depicting acts of a sexual nature, as is the case under Article 5 of the Directive. As for Article 7(d), the premise 'with the aim of inciting others to cause physical harm or serious psychological harm to that person' limits the access to justice by referring to such a specific motivation of the perpetrator. In many cases, the perpetrator will be motivated by another, equally harmful goal, while in others, his motivation will remain undetermined, which would preclude prosecution of the act and punishment of the perpetrator.

Article 8(1) of the Directive, the last of the four provisions on cyberviolence against women, provides for digital incitement to violence or hatred, indicating that it is to be a crime to intentionally incite violence or hatred directed against a group of persons, defined by reference to gender, or against a member of such a group by publicly disseminating by means of information and communication technologies material containing such incitement. In doing so, Article 8(2) allows Member States to decide to criminalize only such acts that either carried out in a manner likely to disturb public order or which are threatening, abusive, or insulting which limits effective response to the various forms of incitement to violence or hatred against women in the online space.

Apart from criminalizing some forms of violence against women, particularly cyberviolence against women in a few of its forms, the Directive addresses violence against women more comprehensively. It includes chapters concerning protection of victims and access to justice (Chapter 3), victim support (Chapter 4), prevention and early intervention (Chapter 5), and coordination and cooperation (Chapter 6).

Article 14 on reporting of violence against women or domestic violence enables victims to report violence online. According to Article 14(1) in addition to the rights of victims when making a complaint under Article 5 of Directive 2012/29/EU, Member States shall ensure that victims can report acts of violence against women or domestic violence to the competent authorities through accessible, easy-to-use, safe, and readily available channels. That shall include, at least for the cybercrimes referred to in Articles 5 to 8 of this Directive, the possibility of reporting online or through other accessible and secure ICT. However, the phrase 'without prejudice to national procedural rules regarding formalising online reporting' located at the end of the regulation allows Member States to leave their procedural rules on online reporting unchanged even if they are not easy-to-use.

Article 15 'Investigation and prosecution' obliges Member States to ensure that persons, units, or services investigating and prosecuting acts of violence against women or domestic violence have adequate expertise in those matters and have effective investigative tools at their disposal to effectively investigate and prosecute such acts, especially for the purpose of gathering, analyzing, and securing electronic evidence in cases of cybercrime as referred to in Articles 5 to 8. Article 36 on training and information for professionals underlines training activities shall be complemented by appropriate follow-up, including on the cybercrimes referred to in Articles 5 to 8, and built on the specificities of violence against women and domestic violence. Such training activities may include training on how to identify and address the specific protection and support needs of victims who face a heightened risk of violence due to their experiencing intersectional discrimination. However, training for some groups of professionals that come into contact with victims is not obligatory according to the Article 36, and Member States are required only to 'offer' or 'promote' such training.

Article 25 states that specialist support services shall provide support to victims of cybercrimes as referred to in Articles 5 to 8, including on how to document the cybercrime and information on judicial remedies and remedies to remove online content related to the crime. Since other articles on the procedure itself have some limitations, providing victims of cybercrime with the knowledge on how to document the crime and what the remedies could be useless. According to Article 34(8) preventive measures shall specifically address the cybercrimes referred to in Articles 5 to 8, particularly include the development of digital literacy skills, including critical engagement with the digital world and critical thinking to enable users to identify and address cases of cyber violence, to seek support and to prevent its perpetration. In addition, Member States shall foster multidisciplinary and stakeholder cooperation, including among relevant intermediary service providers and competent authorities, to develop and implement measures to address the cybercrimes referred to in Articles 5 to 8. Again, the skills concerning identification and addressing cases of cyberviolence are essential, but without concrete obligations of service providers, they could be challenging to use in practice. At the same time, the Article 34(8) doesn't include any obligation for service providers even in terms of cooperation with the authorities. Article 42 on cooperation between intermediary service providers provides that 'Member States shall encourage self-regulatory cooperation between relevant intermediary service providers, such as the establishment of codes of conduct'. This way service providers are not obliged to take any concrete action and should be 'encouraged' to establish codes of conduct that are not sufficient as a measure to protect the victims of cyberviolence.

Article 23 'Measures to remove certain online material' obliges Member States to take the necessary measures to ensure that online publicly accessible material as referred to in Article 5(1), points (a) and (b), and Articles 7 and 8 of this Directive is promptly removed or that access thereto is disabled. Measures shall include the possibility for the competent authorities to issue binding legal orders to remove or to disable access to such material that are addressed to hosting service providers. Where removal would not be feasible, the competent authorities may also address orders to disable access to the material concerned to relevant intermediary service providers other than hosting service providers that have the technical and operational ability to take action regarding the material concerned. Member States shall ensure that the orders and other measures are taken following transparent procedures and are subject to adequate safeguards, in particular to ensure that those orders and other measures are limited to what is necessary and proportionate and that due account is taken of the rights and interests of all relevant parties involved, including their fundamental rights in accordance with the Charter. However, according to Article 23(3) Member States shall ensure that, where criminal proceedings regarding an offense as referred to in Article 5(1), point (a) or (b), Article 7 or Article 8 are terminated without leading to a finding that an offense has been committed, orders are discharged, and the addressees of such orders are informed thereof. As experts underline, it is unclear whether the orders can be applied without criminal report or prosecution. Many jurisdictions now provide for civil orders to be issued to remove non-consensual material, including orders against perpetrators and platforms, as well as regulatory bodies that take-down material on behalf of victims while criminal prosecution and conviction may be a prerequisite in the Directive.[107]

The Directive includes a progressive and pro-victim approach in some parts of the Preamble. It contains a substantive diagnosis of the origin and consequences of cyberviolence and women that are targeted. Recital 17 explains that cyberviolence mainly targets and impacts women politicians, journalists, and human rights defenders and can have the effect of silencing women and hindering their societal participation on an equal footing with men. It notices cyberviolence also disproportionately affects women and girls in educational settings, such as schools and universities, with detrimental consequences to their further education and their mental health, causes social exclusion, anxiety, and inducement to inflict self-harm, and can, in extreme cases, lead to suicide. The Preamble recognizes that the use of ICT bears the risk of easy, fast, and widespread amplification of certain forms of cyberviolence with the clear risk of creating or enhancing profound and long-lasting harm to the victim (Recital 18) and making images, videos, or similar material depicting sexually explicit activities or the intimate parts of a person accessible to the public by means of ICT without that person's consent can be very harmful for victims (Recital 19). It acknowledges cyberstalking is a modern form of violence which is often perpetrated against family members or persons living in the same household as the offender but is also perpetrated by ex-partners or acquaintances in order to intensify coercive and controlling behavior, manipulation, and surveillance, thereby increasing the victim's fear, anxiety, and gradual isolation from friends, family and work (Recital 21). It underlines women are often the target of sexist and misogynous hate online, which can escalate into hate crime offline (Recital 25).

While the Preamble recognizes the seriousness of cyberviolence, it includes disclaimers that are simple limitations of its effectiveness. Recital 20 underlines the need to protect the freedom of expression and justifies the dissemination of materials depicting sexually explicit activities or the intimate parts of a person without that person's consent to the public by means of ICT by the need to safeguarding the freedom of expression. Recital 27 ensures 'a fair balance between the freedom of expression and the prosecution of the offence of cyber incitement to violence or hatred' and punishing only conduct which is carried out in a manner likely to disturb public order or which is threatening, abusive, or insulting. As a consequence, the Directive fails to provide necessary help, protection, and support for victims of cyberviolence, appropriate preventive measures, effective cooperation between service providers and authorities, and the implementation of access to justice.

The opportunity for a comprehensive approach to addressing cyberviolence in the binding EU laws such as regulations and directives has been wasted. Either the regulations and directives presented above don't provide efficient tools to protect victims and prosecute the cyberviolence behaviors, nor the Directive on violence against women even when considered alongside these regulations and directives.

Conclusions

Both states and international organizations are attempting to introduce regulations to combat cyberviolence against women. Regulations adopted at the international level are key, given the cross-border nature of cyberviolence against women. However, there is a lack of comprehensive regulations that address each key area of such laws, such as prevention, protection, and prosecution. The UN, which could play a crucial role in combating cyberviolence against women, ignores the issue in its recent Convention on Cybercrime. The CEDAW Convention and its mechanisms address cyberviolence inefficiently, as does the Council of Europe's Istanbul Convention. However, at least attempts are being made to interpret the latter one to use the law to protect women-victims of cyberviolence. The EU, which pioneered the recent adoption of specific instruments regulating the digital sphere, has failed when it comes to a comprehensive and victim-centered approach, and its laws contain many gaps and limitations.

It's very clear in all approaches that the role of social media platforms is ignored, and there is a reluctance to regulate their obligations to combat harmful content for women. There is no such reluctance when it comes to copyrights or intellectual property, for example. The laws and their application mean that the platforms immediately remove any content that violates copyrights without discussion. Why, in the case of cyberviolence against women and other marginalized groups, is there no such governments' determination and will? Who loses from this approach and who benefits (including financially)?

Notes

1 N. Jankowicz *et al.*, 'Malign creativity. How gender, sex, and lies are weaponized against women online', *Wilson Center*, January 2021, www.wilsoncenter.org/sites/default/files/media/uploads/documents/Report%20Malign%20Creativity%20How%20Gender%2C%20Sex%2C%20and%20Lies%20are%20Weaponized%20Against%20Women%20Online_0.pdf
2 Jankowicz *et al.*, 'Malign creativity'.
3 End Violence against Women Coalition and Glitch UK, 'The ripple effect. COVID-19 and the epidemic of online abuse', 2020, https://glitchcharity.co.uk/covid19/'; see also NORC at the University of Chicago and International Center for Research on Women, 'Landscape analysis of technology-facilitated gender-based violence. Findings from the Asia Region', February 2022, www.icrw.org/wp-content/uploads/2021/09/USAID-TFGBV-Landscape-Analysis-Asia.pdf (access December 6, 2025); O. Jurasz, 'Online violence against women: a four nations study', The Open University, 2024, https://oro.open.ac.uk/96398/.
4 European Parliament, Policy Department for Citizens' Rights and Constitutional Affairs, 'Social media platforms and challenges for democracy, rule of law and fundamental rights', April 2023, www.europarl.europa.eu/RegData/etudes/STUD/2023/743400/IPOL_STU(2023)743400_EN.pdf.
5 S. Spurek, 'Cyberprzemoc wobec kobiet w Polsce. Raport z badan' ('Cyberviolence against women in Poland. Survey report'), 2024, https://sylwiaspurek.pl/
6 Spurek, 'Cyberprzemoc wobec kobiet' ('Cyberviolence against women').
7 European Union Agency for Fundamental Rights, 'Online content moderation. Current challenges in detecting hate speech', 2023, https://fra.europa.eu/sites/default/files/fra_uploads/fra-2023-online-content-moderation_en.pdf (access December 6, 2025).

8 European Union Agency for Fundamental Rights, 'Online content moderation
9 Commission on the Status of Women, CSW67 Agreed Conclusions, 'Innovation and technological change, and education in the digital age for achieving gender equality and the empowerment of all women and girls', 67. Session, March 6–7, 2023, https://documents.un.org/doc/undoc/ltd/n23/081/71/pdf/n2308171.pdf.
10 Council of Europe Commissioner for Human Rights, Dunja Mijatović, 'Safeguarding human rights in the era of artificial intelligence', July 3, 2018, www.coe.int/en/web/commissioner/-/safeguarding-human-rights-in-the-era-of-artificial-intelligence (access December 6, 2025).
11 S.R. O'Brien, N.P. Fernández, '2022 Global Symposium on technology-facilitated gender-based violence results: building a common pathway', Wilson Center and UNFPA, September 27, 2023, www.wilsoncenter.org/publication/2022-global-symposium-technology-facilitated-gender-based-violence-results-building.
12 United Nations Human Rights, 'Report of the Special Rapporteur on violence against women, its causes and consequences on online violence against women and girls from a human rights perspective', June 18, 2018, https://documents.un.org/doc/undoc/gen/g18/184/58/pdf/g1818458.pdf.
13 European Institute for Gender Equality, 'Combating Cyber Violence against women and girls', November 25, 2022, https://eige.europa.eu/publications-resources/publications/combating-cyber-violence-against-women-and-girls.
14 European Institute for Gender Equality, 'Combating Cyber Violence'.
15 European Institute for Gender Equality, 'Combating Cyber Violence'.
16 European Parliament's Policy Department for Citizens' Rights and Constitutional Affairs, 'The legislative frameworks for victims of gender-based violence (including children) in the 27 Member States', October 2022, www.europarl.europa.eu/RegData/etudes/STUD/2022/738126/IPOL_STU(2022)738126_EN.pdf (access December 6, 2025).
17 Council of Europe, 'Cyberviolence. Germany: Regulations for service providers', www.coe.int/en/web/cyberviolence/germany (access December 6, 2025).
18 European Parliament, Policy Department for Citizens' Rights and Constitutional Affairs, 'Social media platforms'.
19 Freedom House, 'Freedom on the net 2024. Germany', 2024, https://freedomhouse.org/country/germany/freedom-net/2024 (access December 6, 2025).
20 Group of Experts on Action against Violence against Women and Domestic Violence (GREVIO), 'Report submitted by Spain pursuant to Article 68, paragraph 1 of the Council of Europe Convention on preventing and combating violence against women and domestic violence (1st thematic evaluation round)', February 13, 2024, https://rm.coe.int/grevio-inf-2024-1-spain-1st-thematic-evaluation-round-eng/1680ae0c38 (access December 6, 2025).
21 C. McGlynn, L. Woods, A. Antoniou, 'Pornography, the Online Safety Act 2023 and the need for further reform', August 18, 2024, https://ssrn.com/abstract=4928796 (access December 6, 2025).
22 McGlynn, Woods, Antoniou, 'Pornography'.
23 A. Flynn, N. Henry, 'Image-Based Sexual Abuse: An Australian Reflection', Women & Criminal Justice 2021/31(4), p. 313–326, https://doi.org/10.1080/08974454.2019.1646190 (access December 6, 2025); T. Kirchengast, T. Crofts, 'The legal and policy contexts of 'revenge porn' criminalisation: the need for multiple approaches', Oxford University Commonwealth Law Journal 2019/19(1), p. 1–29, https://doi.org/10.1080/14729342.2019.1580518 (access December 6, 2025).

24 GenPol – Gender & Policy Insights, 'When Technology Meets Misogyny. Multi-level, intersectional solutions to digital gender-based violence', 2020, www.thewomensorganisation.org.uk/wp-content/uploads/2020/09/When-Technology-Meets-Misogyny-GenPol-Policy-Paper-2.pdf.
25 More on eSafety Commissioner, their powers and competences: www.esafety.gov.au
26 European Parliamentary Research Service, 'Measures to address cyber-violence against women in EU Member States and Canada, UK, US', prepared at the request of MEP S. Spurek, 2024.
27 European Parliamentary Research Service, 'Measures to address cyber-violence'.
28 S. Hinduja, J.W. Patchin, 'Cyberstalking Laws', Cyberbullying Research Center, 2023, https://cyberbullying.org/cyberstalking-laws (access December 6, 2025).
29 See examples of prosecutions of stalking in USA in Cybercrime Convention Committee (T-CY), Working Group on cyberbullying and other forms of online violence, especially against women and children, 'Mapping study on cyberviolence', July 9, 2018, https://rm.coe.int/t-cy-2017-10-cbg-study-provisional/16808c4914.
30 European Parliamentary Research Service, 'Measures to address cyber-violence'.
31 The DEFIANCE Act of 2024, www.durbin.senate.gov/imo/media/doc/defiance_act_of_2024.pdf (access December 6, 2025).
32 The text of the resolution 20/8: https://documents.un.org/doc/resolution/gen/g12/153/25/pdf/g1215325.pdf (access November 15, 2024).
33 The text of the resolution 68/181: https://digitallibrary.un.org/record/764453?v=pdf (access November 15, 2024).
34 The text of the resolution 29/14: https://digitallibrary.un.org/record/802808?v=pdf (access November 15, 2024).
35 The text of the resolution 71/199 https://digitallibrary.un.org/record/858023?v=pdf (access November 15, 2024).
36 The text of the resolution 38/5: www.ohchr.org/en/hr-bodies/hrc/regular-sessions/session38/res-dec-stat (access November 15, 2024).
37 The text of the resolution 49/21: https://digitallibrary.un.org/record/3971994?v=pdf (access November 15, 2024).
38 V. Mishra, 'General Assembly adopts landmark resolution on artificial intelligence', March 21, 2024, https://news.un.org/en/story/2024/03/1147831 (access November 13, 2024).
39 The text of the resolution 17/4: https://digitallibrary.un.org/record/720245?v=pdf (access November 15, 2024).
40 United Nations Human Rights, 'Report of the Special Rapporteur'.
41 The text of Agreed Conclusions of 2013: www.unwomen.org/en/csw/outcomes (access November 15, 2024).
42 The text of Agreed Conclusions of 2023: www.unwomen.org/en/csw/csw67-2023/session-outcomes (access November 15, 2024).
43 More on the Global Digital Compact: www.un.org/techenvoy/global-digital-compact (access November 13, 2024).
44 Treaty Bodies: Committee on the Elimination of Discrimination against Women (CEDAW): www.ohchr.org/en/treaty-bodies/cedaw (access November 15, 2024).

45 The text of General Recommendation No. 19 'Violence against women' of 1992 the CEDAW Committee: https://tbinternet.ohchr.org/_layouts/15/treatybodyexternal/Download.aspx?symbolno=INT%2FCEDAW%2FGEC%2F3731&Lang=en (access November 15, 2024).

46 The text of General Recommendation No. 35 'Gender-based violence against women' of 2017 the CEDAW Committee: www.ohchr.org/en/documents/general-comments-and-recommendations/general-recommendation-no-35-2017-gender-based (access November 15, 2024).

47 See United Nations Human Rights, 'Report of the Special Rapporteur'. The Special Rapporteur on violence against women, including its causes and consequences was appointed by the United Nations Commission on Human Rights in 1994 to recommend measures at the local, national, regional, and international levels to eliminate all forms of violence against women, www.ohchr.org/en/special-procedures/sr-violence-against-women (access November 15, 2024).

48 The text of the ICCPR: www.ohchr.org/en/instruments-mechanisms/instruments/international-covenant-civil-and-political-rights (access November 15, 2024).

49 Joint statement of the Special Rapporteur on the promotion of freedom of expression and the Special Rapporteur on violence against women, including its causes and consequences on March 8, 2017, www.ohchr.org/en/press-releases/2017/03/un-experts-urge-states-and-companies-address-online-gender-based-abuse-warn (access November 15, 2024).

50 The text of the report of the Special Rapporteur on the right to privacy: www.ohchr.org/en/documents/thematic-reports/ahrc3762-report-special-rapporteur-right-privacy (access November 15, 2024).

51 The text of the Convention on the Rights of Persons with Disabilities: www.ohchr.org/en/instruments-mechanisms/instruments/convention-rights-persons-disabilities (access November 15, 2024).

52 More on the UN Convention against Cybercrime: www.unodc.org/unodc/en/cybercrime/convention/home.html (access November 15, 2024).

53 More on the Council of Europe, its history, competences and members: www.coe.int/en/web/portal (access November 15, 2024).

54 The text of the Convention on preventing and combating violence against women and domestic violence: https://rm.coe.int/168008482e (access November 22, 2024).

55 More on the Convention's prevention, protection and prosecution measures: www.coe.int/en/web/istanbul-convention/the-convention-in-brief#{%2211642062%22:[1]} (access November 22, 2024).

56 More on the Convention's prevention, protection and prosecution measures: www.coe.int/en/web/istanbul-convention/the-convention-in-brief#{%2211642062%22:[1]} (access November 24, 2024).

57 More on GREVIO: www.coe.int/en/web/istanbul-convention/grevio (access November 24, 2024).

58 The text of the Explanatory report to the Convention: https://rm.coe.int/1680a48903 (access November 22, 2024).

59 Council of Europe, 'Encouraging the participation of the private sector and the media in the prevention of violence against women and domestic violence: article 17 of the

Istanbul Convention. A collection of papers on the Council of Europe Convention on preventing and combating violence against women and domestic violence', January 2016, https://rm.coe.int/16805970bd (access November 24, 2024).

60 Group of Experts on Action against Violence against Women and Domestic Violence (GREVIO), 'GREVIO General Recommendation No. 1 on the digital dimension of violence against women', October 20, 2021, https://rm.coe.int/grevio-rec-no-on-digital-violence-against-women/1680a49147.

61 Group of Experts on Action against Violence against Women and Domestic Violence (GREVIO), 'GREVIO General Recommendation No. 1.

62 Group of Experts on Action against Violence against Women and Domestic Violence (GREVIO), 'GREVIO General Recommendation No. 1.

63 Group of Experts on Action against Violence against Women and Domestic Violence (GREVIO), 'GREVIO General Recommendation No. 1. The issue of measures directed at perpetrators—beyond prosecution and punishment—is not widely addressed. See also the chapter containing recommendations, which highlights the broader necessity of such measures such as awareness raising campaign and education-corrective treatments.

64 The text of the Convention for the Protection of Human Rights and Fundamental Freedoms: www.coe.int/en/web/human-rights-convention (access November 21, 2024).

65 Application no. 56867/15, https://hudoc.echr.coe.int/rus#{%22itemid%22:[%22001-201342%22]} (access November 21, 2024).

66 Application no. 41261/17, https://hudoc.echr.coe.int/fre#{%22itemid%22:[%22001-194321%22]} (access November 21, 2024).

67 Application no. 2872/02, https://hudoc.echr.coe.int/eng#{%22itemid%22:[%22001-89964%22]} (access November 21, 2024).

68 Dink v. Turkey, 2010, Application no. 2668/07, 6102/08, 30079/08, 7072/09, 7124/09, https://hudoc.echr.coe.int/eng#{%22itemid%22:[%22002-808%22]} (access November 21, 2024).

69 Norwood v. the United Kingdom, 2004, Application no. 23131/03, https://hudoc.echr.coe.int/eng#{%22itemid%22:[%22001-67632%22]} (access November 21, 2024).

70 Application no. 64569/09, https://hudoc.echr.coe.int/fre#{%22itemid%22:[%22001-155105%22]} (access November 21, 2024).

71 The text of The Convention on Cybercrime of the Council of Europe: www.coe.int/en/web/cybercrime/the-budapest-convention (access November 21, 2024).

72 The text of the First Additional Protocol to the Convention on Cybercrime of 2003: www.coe.int/en/web/conventions/full-list?module=treaty-detail&treatynum=189 (access November 21, 2024).

73 See A. van der Wilk, 'Protecting women and girls from violence in the digital age. The relevance of the Istanbul convention and the budapest convention on cybercrime in addressing online and technology-facilitated violence against women', Council of Europe, 2021, https://edoc.coe.int/en/violence-against-women/10686-protecting-women-and-girls-from-violence-in-the-digital-age.html.

74 Cybercrime Convention Committee (T-CY), Working Group on cyberbullying and other forms of online violence, especially against women and children, 'Mapping study'.

75 Cybercrime Convention Committee (T-CY), Working Group on cyberbullying and other forms of online violence, especially against women and children, 'Mapping study'.

76 The text of Recommendation CM/Rec(2014)6: www.coe.int/en/web/freedom-expression/committee-of-ministers-adopted-texts/-/asset_publisher/aDXmrol0vvsU/content/recommendation-cm-rec-2014-6-of-the-committee-of-ministers-to-member-states-on-a-guide-to-human-rights-for-internet-users-adopted-by-the-committee-of- (access November 21, 2024).

77 The text of Resolution 2144 (2017): https://assembly.coe.int/nw/xml/XRef/Xref-XML2HTML-en.asp?fileid=23457&lang=en (access November 21, 2024).

78 The Text of Recommendation CM/Rec(2018)2: https://search.coe.int/cm#{%22CoEIdentifier%22:[%2209000016807 90e14%22],%22sort%22:[%22CoEValidationDate%20Descending%22]} (access November 21, 2024).

79 The text of Recommendation CM/Rec(2019)1: https://rm.coe.int/cm-rec-2019-1-on-preventing-and-combating-sexism/168094d894 (access November 21, 2024).

80 The text of Recommendation CM/Rec(2022)16: www.coe.int/en/web/combating-hate-speech/recommendation-on-combating-hate-speech (access November 21, 2024).

81 Committee of Experts on combating technology-facilitated violence against women and girls: www.coe.int/en/web/genderequality/committee-of-experts-on-combating-technology-facilitated-violence-against-women-and-girls-gec/pc-evio-1 (access September 19, 2025).

82 See the overview of EU legal and policy framework on cyberviolence against women in: European Parliament, Policy Department for Citizens' Rights and Constitutional Affairs, 'Cyber violence and hate speech online against women', September 2018, www.europarl.europa.eu/RegData/etudes/STUD/2018/604979/IPOL_STU(2018)604979_EN.pdf; European Parliamentary Research Service, 'Combating gender-based violence: cyber violence. European added value assessment', March 2021, www.europarl.europa.eu/RegData/etudes/STUD/2021/662621/EPRS_STU(2021)662621_EN.pdf; European Institute for Gender Equality, 'Combating Cyber Violence'; European Parliament, Policy Department for Citizens' Rights and Constitutional Affairs, 'Social media platforms'; and European Parliament's Policy Department for Citizens' Rights and Constitutional Affairs, 'The impact of the use of social media on women and girls', March 2023, www.europarl.europa.eu/RegData/etudes/STUD/2023/743341/IPOL_STU(2023)743341_EN.pdf.

83 The text of the GDPR: https://eur-lex.europa.eu/eli/reg/2016/679/oj (access November 21, 2024).

84 Similar provisions concerning protecting privacy and security of personal data in electronic communications were included in the Directive 2009/136/EC of the European Parliament and of the Council of November 25, 2009, amending Directive 2002/22/EC on universal service and users' rights relating to electronic communications networks and services, Directive 2002/58/EC concerning the processing of personal data and the protection of privacy in the electronic communications sector and Regulation (EC) No 2006/2004 on cooperation between national authorities responsible for the enforcement of consumer protection laws so-called the ePrivacy Directive.

85 The text of the DSA: https://eur-lex.europa.eu/eli/reg/2022/2065/oj (access November 21, 2024).

86 The text of the Regulation on e-Evidence: https://eur-lex.europa.eu/eli/reg/2023/1543/oj (access November 21, 2024).

87 The text of the Artificial Intelligence Act: https://eur-lex.europa.eu/eli/reg/2024/1689/oj (access November 21, 2024).
88 The text of the Victims' Rights Directive: https://eur-lex.europa.eu/eli/dir/2012/29/oj (access November 21, 2024).
89 S. Spurek, 'Analysis of the Victims' Rights Directive from a gender perspective', European Institute for Gender Equality, April 16, 2016, https://eige.europa.eu/publications-resources/publications/analysis-victims-rights-directive-gender-perspective?language_content_entity=en (access November 06, 2024).
90 More on the evaluation of the European Commission of the Victims' Rights Directive: https://commission.europa.eu/system/files/2022-06/swd_2022_179_evaluation_rep_en.pdf (access November 06, 2024).
91 The text of Audiovisual Media Services Directive: https://eur-lex.europa.eu/eli/dir/2018/1808/oj (access November 06, 2024).
92 The text of the resolution on strengthening media freedom: https://eur-lex.europa.eu/legal-content/EN/TXT/?uri=CELEX%3A52020IP0320 (access November 06, 2024).
93 The text of the resolution with recommendations to the Commission on identifying gender-based violence as a new area of crime listed in Article 83(1) TFEU: https://eur-lex.europa.eu/legal-content/EN/TXT/?uri=CELEX%3A52021IP0388 (access November 06, 2024).
94 The text of the resolution with recommendations to the Commission on combating gender-based violence: cyberviolence: https://eur-lex.europa.eu/legal-content/EN/TXT/?uri=CELEX%3A52021IP0489 (access November 06, 2024).
95 The text of the Gender Equality Strategy 2020–2025: https://ec.europa.eu/newsroom/just/items/682425/en (access November 06, 2024).
96 The text of the Strategy on Victims' Rights 2020–2025: https://eur-lex.europa.eu/legal-content/EN/TXT/?uri=CELEX%3A52020DC0258 (access November 06, 2024).
97 The Code and its evaluation documents: https://commission.europa.eu/strategy-and-policy/policies/justice-and-fundamental-rights/combatting-discrimination/racism-and-xenophobia/eu-code-conduct-countering-illegal-hate-speech-online_en (access November 06, 2024).
98 A. van der Wilk, 'Protecting women and girls'.
99 A. Brown, 'Models of Governance of Online Hate Speech', Council of Europe, 2020, https://edoc.coe.int/en/fundamental-freedoms/10357-models-of-governance-of-online-hate-speech.html (access November 06, 2024).
100 More on the evaluation on the Code of Conduct on Countering Illegal Hate Speech Online: https://commission.europa.eu/strategy-and-policy/policies/justice-and-fundamental-rights/combatting-discrimination/racism-and-xenophobia/eu-code-conduct-countering-illegal-hate-speech-online_en (access November 06, 2024).
101 C. Rigotti, C. McGlynn, 'Towards an EU criminal law on violence against women: the ambitions and limitations of the commission's proposal to criminalise image-based sexual abuse', New Journal of European Criminal Law 2022/13(4), pp. 452–477, https://doi.org/10.1177/20322844221140713.
102 'Bumble and Safety Experts Call for EU to Ban Cyberflashing and A.I. Image Abuse', https://bumble-buzz.com/bumble-cyberflashing-ai-eu-policy/ (access November 01, 2024).

103 Bumble and Safety Experts Call for EU to Ban Cyberflashing and A.I. Image Abuse', https://bumble-buzz.com/bumble-cyberflashing-ai-eu-policy/ (access November 01, 2024).

104 Opinion of European Economic and Social Committee, 'Combating Violence against Women', 2022, www.eesc.europa.eu/en/our-work/opinions-information-reports/opinions/combatting-violence-against-women (access October 17, 2024).

105 C. Rigotti, C. McGlynn, 'Towards an EU criminal law on violence against women'.

106 C. Rigotti, C. McGlynn, 'Image-Based Sexual Abuse and EU Law: A Critical Analysis', German Law Journal 2024, www.cambridge.org/core/journals/german-law-journal/article/imagebased-sexual-abuse-and-eu-law-a-critical-analysis/B0CF334A0037DE3CA2067B79F506EB87 (access February 1, 2025).

107 C. Rigotti, C. McGlynn, 'Image-Based Sexual Abuse'.

3 Recommendations

Introduction

There is no doubt the first step for States should be to recognize cyberviolence against women as a human rights violation and a form of discrimination and GBV against women, review existing laws, ratify and duly apply core international human rights instruments to prevent, protect, and prosecute cyberviolence against women. Women's human rights that are protected offline should be protected online, too.

The second and crucial step is, however, developing a common international legislative framework to fight cross-border and transnational cyberviolence against women. The reports, studies, and analysis show existing legislative frameworks are fragmented, outdated, and poorly implemented. Women are not protected from cyberviolence, prevention measures are rarely in place, and the perpetrators are not held accountable. The scale, harms, and consequences of cyberviolence against women show a pressing need to revise current legislation and draft the law that could create an effective mechanism for preventing the violence, for seeking justice for victims and for holding perpetrators accountable and unlearn their violent behaviors (through education-corrective measures). There is a need to create a global law since only such law could address the cross-border nature of cyberviolence.

As in the case of offline forms of violence against women, in combating violence against women, measures on the so-called 3Ps should be implemented: prevention, protection, and prosecution. All measures should be coordinated and the cooperation of all relevant actors should be ensured. Data collection and research should be conducted to understand the phenomenon better and undertake appropriate legislative interventions. As gender-based discrimination and exclusion of women are part of the problem and root causes of the cyberviolence, we propose some measures on the achievement of gender equality, but only regarding the digital sphere since. There are commonly agreed measures on gender equality that experts have talked about for years.

DOI: 10.4324/9781003683193-4

The set of recommendations indicated below was created based on the existing reports, research, and analysis. We made use of already developed recommendations prepared by the United Nations bodies and institutions, agencies of regional organizations such as the Council of Europe and the EU, and NGOs, CSOs, and experts' reports that have already undertaken advocacy efforts. We also carefully analyzed binding and soft laws and prepared recommendations based on the existing legal provisions. The set of recommendations is the first ever attempt to collect existing recommendations on combating cyberviolence against women of various organizations and institutions (see the list of the laws, soft laws and reports in the Annex). They were compiled with some recommendations of the book's author.

The recommendations are addressed to legislators and include the governments' obligations. The separate recommendations refer to obligations of the platforms and intermediaries to be included in the laws. The prevention and protection measures, the measures on prosecution, coordination and cooperation, and accountability of the platforms should be introduced in the binding laws and duly enforced. Since cyberviolence against women constantly evolves, the efficiency of the adopted laws should be monitored, and the laws should be revised if necessary. Someone could say no law is perfect. However, we can draft the laws that keep system errors to a minimum, discourage harmful behavior, and react when cyberviolence occurs by protecting the victim, punishing the perpetrator, and holding accountable all other responsible entities.

Recommendations on prevention

To prevent violence against women by addressing its root causes and working to change attitudes, gender roles, stereotypes, and sexist attitudes that make violence against women, including cyberviolence acceptable, governments should:

[Gender equality]

1 Foster gender equality in society and support the empowerment and representation of women online.
2 Take measures to eliminate any gender inequality in access to technologies.
3 Promote more girls and women in STEM and in technology and AI education, careers, and business, ensure that they acquire the knowledge and skills to attain high-quality jobs in the digital and sustainable economy, particularly by promoting and investing in gender-responsive, quality, equitable and inclusive education, lifelong learning, reskilling, and vocational training and studies, and ensuring that women and girls diversify their educational and occupational choices in emerging fields, such as science, technology, engineering, arts and mathematics, and ICT, and acquire digital skills.
4 Increase and bring to positions of parity women coders, developers, and decision-makers, with intersectionality in mind.

5 Ensure the full, equal, and meaningful participation and leadership of women in the digital and technology sectors, including in policy, regulatory, and governance processes.
6 Promote the full, equal, and meaningful participation and leadership of young women and, as appropriate, adolescent girls, in decision-making processes in the context of innovation and technological change, and education in the digital age.
7 Take measures to protect and promote the rights of all women and girls with disabilities, including by addressing all barriers that prevent or restrict their full, equal, and meaningful participation in the design, management, resourcing, and implementation of ICT policies, ensuring their access to disability-inclusive and accessible digital information and technology, digital literacy, and skills.
8 Promote the equal access of women in the rural areas, older women, Indigenous women, migrant women, and women of different groups by addressing the multiple and intersecting forms of discrimination and barriers they face, ensuring access to quality and inclusive education, the Internet, and digital services.

[Measures addressed to boys]

1 Encourage men and boys to abandon harmful stereotypes of women and men and to adopt respectful and healthy behaviors in the digital sphere.
2 Engage men and boys in awareness-raising activities to make them question and recognize issues of patriarchy and cultural or social norms that are harmful to themselves and others and to help them understand what cyberviolence against women is, how it is harmful, and how to prevent it.
3 Encourage men and boys to be positive role models, allies, and agents of change for gender equality, promote respectful relationships, and refrain from and condemn all forms of violence against all women and girls in the digital spheres, while ensuring that they take responsibility and are held accountable for their behavior online and offline, including for behavior that perpetuates gender stereotypes and negative social norms.
4 Dedicate funding to interventions focused on preempting radicalization of men and boys in online spaces and supporting their deradicalization.

[Awareness raising campaigns]

1 Design, implement, and promote regular national awareness-raising to eliminate negative social norms and gender stereotypes and allocate resources to finance effective awareness-raising campaigns.
2 Implement awareness-raising campaign that aim to increase understanding of the links between sexism, lack of gender equality and violence against

women and girls, different forms of violence against women perpetrated online, how to prevent it, of the harm the cyberviolence generate for individuals and society, the legal rights of the victims, and the support services available to victims.

3 Implement awareness-raising through diverse forms of media (e.g., the production of handbooks, guidelines, and video clips available on the Internet and in mainstream media, the introduction of a national day against sexism, and the setting up of museums to celebrate gender equality and women's rights).
4 Target the general public but also five main specific groups of audiences of awareness-raising campaigns:

- groups at risk of experiencing cyberviolence against women, including prominent and high-profile women in the public eye, women's human rights defenders, feminists, activists, and individuals working for organizations seeking to address gender inequality, nonbinary people;
- groups in positions able to offer support to those at risk of experiencing cyberviolence against women;
- groups in positions to enforce legislation (law enforcement, judges, lawyers);
- parents/caregivers, teachers, community groups, NGOs/CSOs;
- groups who are potential perpetrators of cyberviolence against women.

[Training]

1 Provide mandatory, tailored, and continuous capacity building, education, and training for all relevant professionals, including but not limited to law-enforcement professionals, criminal justice actors, members of the judiciary (especially to first responders in the police and the justice sectors), healthcare professionals, asylum officials, social service professionals, and education professionals, journalists, to equip them with knowledge on digital expressions of violence against women, responding to women and girls as victims without causing secondary victimization and re-traumatization.
2 Integrate the issue of cyberviolence against women into general training for law enforcement and judicial personnel.
3 Introduce training activities with a gender and intersectional perspective.

[Digital literacy]

1 Promote digital literacy in the use of the Internet and ICT for all, without sex- or gender-based discrimination.
2 Provide gender-sensitive trainings for Internet users on cyberviolence against women and girls in schools and communities as a way to prevent it.

3 Implement training programs to increase the digital, data, and media literacy and skills of all women and girls, as well as those with disabilities, throughout their life course, focusing on their empowerment and building confidence and trust for use, including skills to use and understand technology, search for, share and manage information, build knowledge and awareness of their rights and online risk mitigation.

[Education]

1 Include online safety, gender equality, human rights, and education on media in formal curricula and teaching materials at all levels of education, both public and private, from early childhood.
2 Ensure curricula and teaching materials enable learners to learn about equality between women and men, non-stereotyped gender roles, mutual respect, non-violent conflict resolution in interpersonal relationships, and violence against women, cyberviolence in particular, including the risks of taking, or allowing others to take, intimate images, and that the dissemination of such images is a form of GBV.
3 Make teaching materials accessible to persons with physical and/or intellectual disabilities.
4 Ensure curricula contain age-appropriate, evidence-based, and scientifically accurate, and comprehensive sex and sexuality education for girls and boys.
5 Ensure the assessment of textbooks, training materials and teaching methods used by/for students of all age groups and in all forms of education and training (starting with preschool education) for sexist language, illustrations, and gender stereotypes and revise them so that they actively promote gender equality.
6 Establish and promote programs (including software) for children, young people, parents, and educators to assist in advising children on media literacy for a safe and critical use of digital media and appropriate digital behavior.
7 Involve women's rights experts and practitioners in both curricula and teaching material development, as well as training of teachers, parents, and other figures with pastoral care responsibilities to make sure that educational programs successfully counteract the sexist stereotypes and discriminatory attitudes that inform violence in all its manifestations.
8 Incorporate training on new-technology-facilitated violence against women into university curricula for law, psychology, health care, and social work degrees.

[Other measures]

1 Oblige media organizations and journalists unions, traditional and online media, to take concrete steps to eradicate gender-based discrimination, victim-blaming attitudes, and violations of the privacy of victims of GBV

against women and to promote positive and non-stereotypical portrayals of women and men in the media and advertising.

2 Ban sexist hate speech and patriarchal stereotypes in media.
3 Oblige media to moderate online debates in a transparent manner and provide users with clear guidelines for online debates, complaints, and reports on cyberviolence (see moderation and complaints standards in the section of the recommendations for the platforms).
4 Oblige all employers to adopt a workplace policy on GBV and harassment, including cyberviolence, put in place specific training to make their employees feel as safe online as possible, conduct a robust risk assessment in relation to cyberviolence against women at work, and take measures to prevent it.
5 Incorporate digital manifestations of violence against women in any existing intervention programs for perpetrators of violence (education-corrective measures), in particular in the context of intimate-partner and domestic violence.
6 Assess the impact of all relevant projects funded by public funds on the implications for protection of women from cyberviolence.
7 Assess all relevant draft laws on the effect on the protection of women from cyberviolence.

Recommendations on protection and support

1 Provide support to women-victims of cyberviolence, including social, healthcare, short and long-term psychological counseling, and legal services, helplines, and protection orders.
2 Provide prompt, adequate, and free of charge support services.
3 Equip support services with the financial and human resources to offer holistic services.
4 Provide support through a variety of means, without excessive formalities and through a sufficient geographical distribution to allow all women-victims of cyberviolence the opportunity to access such services.
5 Whether managed by governmental services or women's organizations, ensure deep understanding of the support services of the continuum of violence against women and girls; the response should be gender-sensitive and integrate the specificities of the digital dimension of violence against women.
6 Ensure that the services apply an intersectional perspective.
7 Ensure that the services include all forms of violence committed in the digital sphere and all women-victims of cyberviolence, including such violence perpetrated in the context of domestic violence.
8 Provide training for all frontline workers to ensure their ability to support victims of cyberviolence; they should receive both general and specialist training to a level appropriate to their contact with victims to increase their awareness of the needs of victims and to enable them to deal with victims in an impartial, respectful, and professional manner (see also recommendations on the prevention regarding training for professionals).

9 Develop specialized, precise, efficient, and transparent internal and external protocols and codes of conduct for frontline workers addressing cyberviolence against women so that officials can provide a timely, adequate, and accessible response to this form of violence.
10 Develop and widely disseminate accessible information on the support services available to victims of cyberviolence against women; a regularly updated directory and list of support services should be made available to increase awareness of available remedies.
11 Allow victims to obtain protection orders to prevent their abusers from posting or sharing intimate images without their consent or engaging in another form of harassment or violence, whether online or offline.
12 Ensure that the protection measures encompass the establishment of procedures for the immediate removal of gender-based harmful content through the elimination of the original material or its distribution.
13 Ensure that emergency barring orders and protection orders are responsive to forms of domestic violence perpetrated online or via ICT and to other digital manifestations of violence against women.
14 Empower equality bodies and ombuds institutions, which have a mandate to work on gender equality and non-discrimination, to address the digital dimension of violence against women from the point of view of the structural discrimination and barrier to the realization of women's human rights, which it may represent.
15 Ensure women's organizations supporting victims of cyberviolence and the survivors' support networks are sustainably funded.
16 Ensure employers develop support policies for women employees facing cyberviolence, including mental health services, support for employees or affiliates' legal fees and other expenses (such as anti-doxxing service subscriptions), and outlining precise mechanisms for targets to report such campaigns against them to official communications and human resources staff. This especially applies to fields where women (generally in public-facing roles) are particularly exposed to cyberviolence, such as political parties, media companies, and news agencies.

Recommendations on prosecution and punishment

In order to ensure that victims of cyberviolence against women have adequate access to criminal justice systems and that the authorities adequately respond to such cases, establishing legal mechanisms that combat cyberviolence against women, allow for diligent investigation and punishment of acts of online violence against women, and bringing perpetrators to justice for their actions

[What to combat]

1 The legislation should prohibit and criminalize online violence against women, in particular the non-consensual distribution of intimate images, online harassment and stalking, and hate speech.
2 The criminalization of online violence against women should encompass all elements of this type of abuse, including subsequent 're-sharing' of harmful content.
3 The threat to disseminate non-consensual images must be made illegal so that advocates and prosecutors may intervene before abuse is perpetrated.
4 The use of information and communication technologies should be clearly mentioned, and the specific forms and impacts of digital forms of violence should be addressed appropriately.
5 The legislation should highlight the continuum between online and offline manifestations of violence, allowing the identification of cases in which the violence starts in the digital sphere and continues in the physical world (or vice versa, in particular in domestic violence cases).
6 The legislation should prevent commercial entities from making profit out of sexual abuse of women and girls constituting sexual violence, such as filmed rape, including by criminalizing the production and distribution of such content.
7 The legislation should incorporate a gender and intersectional aspect to address cyberviolence against women as acts of GBV.

[Who to be punished]

Both primary perpetrators and re-transmitters should be held responsible for the re-transmission of violating materials, to hold secondary perpetrators of violence accountable, too.

[How to prosecute the case]

1 Ensure access to justice, including promoting awareness of reporting mechanisms.
2 Create online and offline complaints mechanisms within law enforcement and prosecution services that are easily and immediately accessible to victims, including those with physical as well as intellectual and psychosocial disabilities.
3 Equip law enforcement and other criminal justice actors with the necessary human, financial, and technical resources to effectively investigate and prosecute cyberviolence against women, particularly to develop their forensic capabilities on the collecting and securing electronic evidence. This may include creating specialist units and facilitating the co-ordination and co-operation

of such units with existing cybercrime units/experts and specialized training for frontline workers (see also recommendations on protection measures regarding training of professionals).

4 Ensure that women-victims of cyberviolence are offered all necessary information, without unnecessary delay, from their first contact with a competent authority to enable them to access their rights, including information on the support and protection measures, the procedures and their role in the procedures, the law enforcement contact details for communications about their case.
5 Ensure the publication of incidence reports by the criminal justice sector on cyberviolence against women and additional information on arrests, indictments, convictions, and sentences as well as information on sex, age, type of violence as well as the relationship of the perpetrator to the victim, geographical location, and other factors deemed relevant with a view to strengthening the confidence of victims in the criminal justice system.

[International cooperation]

Enhance international co-operation and mutual legal assistance capacities of criminal justice actors in matters related to the cyberviolence against women to collect, secure, and disclose evidence of cybercrimes directed at women, particularly the identification of perpetrators (including ensuring simplified access to evidence held by service providers, e.g. subscriber information to identify the owner of an account or an IP address used in the commission of an offence).

[Penalties]

Impose adequate, necessary, and proportional penalties to the criminal act. The certainty of adequate punishment conveys the message that cyberviolence against women and girls is not tolerated to combat the culture of impunity of perpetrators.

[Reparation measures]

1 Ensure reparations that should include financial compensation to cover the costs of the quantifiable losses incurred (such as the cost of medical care, loss of wages and income, and damage to property), injuries and non-quantifiable losses, in addition to the need for survivors to rebuild their lives in the short, medium and long terms.
2 Ensure reparation measures include the immediate removal of the harmful content and forms of restitution, rehabilitation, satisfaction, and guarantees of non-repetition, depending on the circumstances and the preferences of the victim. They should also include an immediate injunction to prevent the publication of harmful content.

Recommendations on coordination and cooperation

1 Ensure coordination of measures at all levels of government and by all relevant public agencies and institutions, involving government agencies, national, regional, and local parliaments and authorities, equality and ombuds institutions, national statistics offices.
2 Allocate appropriate human and financial resources to national and local bodies, as well as to healthcare and social protection institutions, to implement coordinated laws and policies on cyberviolence against women. The resources should be sufficient to enable these bodies and institutions to call in IT experts, obtain technical equipment, and build digital infrastructure as necessary.
3 Adopt and implement budgeted national action plan on combating cyberviolence against women or ensure recognition of the digital dimension of violence against women in national strategies, programs, and action plans on violence against women as part of a holistic response to all forms of violence against women.
4 Ensure recognition of the digital dimension of violence against women in other strategies, programs, or action plans on digitalization, cybercrime, and security.
5 Create an independent body to address cyberviolence against women, or clearly assign the tasks on this to the existing one, including offering legal remedies and supporting individuals, conducting research, and awareness-raising campaigns.
6 Ensure participation and multi-stakeholder cooperation, including stakeholders from different sectors (academia, government, civil society, private sector) and disciplines (technology, data, gender equality, ethics, human rights), mainly by providing resources and an enabling environment for the creation of effective public–private partnerships involving public authorities and the private and ICT sector, NGOs, and civil society actors (particularly women's organizations and specialist service providers).
7 Work closely with and consult women's rights organizations and experts on cyberviolence against women and people with intersecting identities, including women in the technology workforce, in STEM movements and those working on gender equality and women's and girls' empowerment in specific contexts (access to justice, economic empowerment, ending violence against women, support for victims, education, health, awareness raising, etc.); cooperation and consultations should include the conception, planning, adoption, implementation, monitoring, and evaluation of laws and policies on cyberviolence against women.
8 Ensure stable and adequate funding for civil society and women's rights organizations, particularly for advocacy and watchdog NGOs that serve as a counterweight to considerable tech companies lobbying.

9 Ensure funding for technology startups founded by women, scholarships for women studying in the field of STEM, and women researchers.

Recommendations on data and research

1 Establish a system to systematically collect and analyze disaggregated data on violence against women with a digital component, including the number of reported cases, the number of prosecuted cases, the number of condemnations and conviction rates, the average time lapse in responding to each report, the type of Police action taken in disposing cases including the number of arrests, as well as data on the civil justice measures imposed, such as restraining orders. All data should be gathered and analyzed through an intersectional lens and disaggregated by the type of violence, age, and relationship between perpetrator and victim(s), the type of cyber violence experienced, potential aggravating circumstances (the number of perpetrators, length of abuse, permanence of data, existence of overlapping forms of violence, involvement of or impact on the victim's children, etc.), and other relevant factors.
2 Ensure that data on suicides or suicide attempts and femicides include information on the history of violence perpetrated in the digital sphere.
3 Disseminate widely such data on a regular basis to the relevant public authorities, education establishments, and the public.
4 Strengthen the capacity and coordination of national statistics and data production offices, government institutions and other public research organizations to collect, analyze, disseminate statistics, and data on cyberviolence against women.
5 Undertake or support surveys, research programs, and studies on cyberviolence against women on the prevalence and impacts of TFGBV, to measure the financial, personal, and social implications of such violence, including self-censorship and digital exclusion, to understand the phenomenon and its intersection with emerging technologies, on the evaluation of current initiatives, laws, and policies and measuring their effectiveness, including through in-depth, empirical and interdisciplinary law and policy research, and quantitative and qualitative research that examines system responses, based on a victims' perspective.
6 Ensure the surveys and research include experiences of high-risk groups such as the LGBTQI+ community, gender rights defenders/activists, and women in the public eye to capture the identity and categories of survivors.
7 Foster collaboration among stakeholders, including national statistics offices, research and academic institutions, civil society, and digital technology companies, to assess data needs and address gaps while applying ethical research principles.

Recommendations on platforms and intermediaries

[International human rights framework]

1 Regulations on platforms and Internet intermediaries should respect the international human rights framework, including that with regard to business and human rights, including women's human rights instruments that prohibit gender-based discrimination and gender-based online violence.
2 Platforms and intermediaries should be obliged by the law to cooperate with the treaty bodies and the special procedures actively.

[Campaigns and CSR – the platforms should]

1 Introduce equality and diversity policies, programs, and specific initiatives surrounding women's and digital rights and cyberviolence.
2 Engage in and promote targeted age- and gender-sensitive efforts to promote the awareness of all users of their rights and freedoms in the digital environment, both vis-à-vis States and intermediaries, including, in particular information about applicable complaint mechanisms and procedures.
3 Allocate resources to information and education campaigns on preventing cyberviolence against women and girls and on promoting human rights and digital security.
4 Adopt internal gender equality commitments.

[Design]

1 Avoid gender bias in the design of all their products.
2 Implement gender-responsive, age-, and disability-inclusive approaches and include human rights perspective in technology design, development, and deployment.
3 Use participatory and feminist approaches to develop and apply technologies and digital platforms, in partnership with women, organizations, and women's rights advocates.
4 Create internal monitoring mechanisms toward ensuring the inclusion of female users and victim-centric perspectives, in particular those exposed to or at risk of intersecting forms of discrimination and violence.
5 Ensure design features of technology enable women's safety online, and accessible reporting options, as well as access to support.
6 Design and implement changes and other interventions which aim to proactively discourage and prevent the occurrence of cyberviolence against women, including online hate speech, harassment, and other systemic risks, as an addition to moderating or removing content, retroactively.
7 Take proactive steps to include women and girls in the planning, coding, and design, particularly by including women and girls in innovation teams.

[Risk assessment and risk mitigation]

1 Conduct regular human rights due diligence, assessing their direct and indirect human rights impact, evaluating the gender-related risks, and defining mitigation measures.
2 Ensure appropriate follow-up to these assessments by acting upon the findings, and monitoring and evaluating the effectiveness of identified responses.
3 While conducting assessment, analyze the frequency, patterns, and causes of complaints received to learn lessons to improve their policies, procedures, and practices and prevent future grievances.
4 Cooperate with NGOs and independent experts to allow them to conduct neutral third-party assessments.

[Terms and conditions of service]

1 Establish, communicate, and enforce strict codes of conduct for users in terms and conditions of service to combat cyberviolence against women.
2 Ensure that all terms and conditions of service agreements and policies specifying the rights of users and all other standards and practices for content moderation and the processing and disclosure of user data are publicly available in clear, plain language, and accessible formats.
3 Notify users in advance of all changes in relevant terms and conditions of service as applicable and without delay, and in formats that they can easily access and understand, including explanatory guides.
4 Regularly review and update terms and conditions of service to address new trends, patterns, and manifestations of violence against women and people with intersecting identities.
5 Empower users to engage in processes of drafting, applying, evaluating, reviewing, and revising terms and conditions of service.
6 Don't include in the terms and conditions of service waivers of rights or hindrances to the effective access to remedies, such as mandatory jurisdiction outside of a user's country of residence or non-derogable arbitration clauses.

[Moderation measures]

1 Introduce swift and effective content moderation of online content as a means of preventing all forms of cyberviolence against women and girls.
2 Publish a clear and comprehensive content moderation policy.
3 Invest in and resource a content moderation and invest more resources in human content moderation.
4 Provide content moderators with initial and regular training on cyberviolence – the nature, extent, forms, roots and consequences, and on the applicable laws and international human rights standards on combating cyberviolence against women.

5 Provide additional training for content moderators that addresses cultural and language barriers, power dynamics, and issues such as gender bias, LGBTQI+ sensitivity, and how cyberviolence targets women and users with intersecting identities.
6 Provide content moderators with clear guidelines to exclude sexism and ensure respect for women's rights.
7 Establish adequate moderation staff and technical resources for all languages which are widely spoken in markets where they operate and hire more speakers of languages that are currently under-represented among content moderators.
8 Assess the human rights impact of automated content management and ensure human review where appropriate.
9 Use various software-based mechanisms to suitably moderate the content and ensure that the safety of their users is respected and to sanction abusive comments.
10 Improve automated detection and update machine learning models using successful reports that individual users have submitted to the platform, as these are ideal examples of human-identified problematic content.
11 Share information and systems to eradicate cross-platform abuse and ensure an automatic content removal that extends across parent, subsidiary, or sibling platforms.
12 Introduce nudges or friction to discourage users from posting abusive content, e.g., informing people that, if they repeatedly violate the rules, their user accounts could be disabled, nudging users to read articles before sharing them.
13 Regularly update platform classifiers or keywords to reflect and root out malign creativity.
14 Provide users with greater control and filters over their online experiences to ensure that they have greater decision-making power over the type of content they see on social media and which users can communicate with them.

[Complaints system]

1 Build and develop content reporting mechanisms, including notice-based procedures.
2 Provide accessible, transparent, user-friendly, and easy to find reporting mechanisms.
3 Ensure that all users have complete and easy access to information about applicable complaint mechanisms, the various stages of the procedure, indicative time frames, and expected outcomes.
4 Ensure reporting mechanisms are made accessible in all languages, in local languages in particular, in clear and understandable language, and to all, including persons with disabilities.

5 Increase the speed of response and respond to reports and complaints in a timely manner.
6 Keep the user informed about the progress of their matter.
7 Analyze the account generating the content, as well as the network accounts disseminating or engaging with harmful content.
8 Implement features that will reduce the number of users that engage with the content.
9 Respond to reports and complaints by taking into account factors that expose women and girls disproportionately to online abuse, notably sex, gender, race, color, language, religion, political or other opinion, national or social origin, association with a national minority, property, birth, sexual orientation, gender identity, age, state of health, disability, marital status, migrant or refugee status, or other status.
10 Allow survivors to confidently report to a CSO/NGO with whom they may be familiar, ensuring that the survivor receives the necessary and appropriate support following their report.
11 Make available effective remedies and dispute resolution systems that provide prompt and direct redress in cases of user, content provider, and affected party grievances, including an impartial and independent review of the alleged violation resulting in inquiry, explanation, reply, correction, apology, deletion, reconnection, or compensation.
12 Swiftly remove harmful content without the need for a court order.
13 Identify repeat offenders and make it more difficult for accounts that have been banned from platforms to resurface (e.g., IP addresses linked to permanently deleted accounts should not be able to recreate accounts for a significant time).
14 Allow users to compile incident reports that provide more context and a more holistic view of the abuse they are experiencing, to add multiple pieces or streams of content from multiple accounts over time, documenting not just a single moment of a campaign against them, but its broader architecture and impact.
15 For high-profile political candidates, journalists, and academics – work with individual targets (or their staff) to identify the unique narratives, nicknames, and memes employed against them and reflect such malign creativity in classifiers and keywords that drive platform content moderation, whether automated or human.
16 Be responsible for the harm caused by a failure to act on harmful material. This means taking economic responsibility for the harm caused to survivors, as well as ensuring enforcement of effective prevention and response mechanisms.

[Measures against perpetrators]

1 Hold perpetrators of gender-based cyberviolence to account by removing the perpetrator from the platform, removal of cyberviolence against women

content, and case referral or reporting of any crime which violates online platforms' rules of conduct.

2 Implement safety mechanisms to prohibit perpetrators from hiding behind the safety net of anonymity.
3 Hold perpetrators of gender-based cyberviolence to account by sanctioning of perpetrators consistent with other platforms' violations.
4 Create and enforce transparent and meaningful consequences for persistent abusers, e.g. a tiered escalation system on repeat offenders targeting marginalized groups, including women. Consequences might include locking and placing a public notice on abusive accounts for a period of time; zeroing out the followers/members/subscribers of an abusive account or group, and de-platforming.

[Obligations on personal data of users]

1 Apply standards for data collection, processing, use, storage, sharing, retention, archiving and deletion, aligned with technological advancement on an ongoing and evolving basis, especially to ensure the protection of women's and girls' personal data, in full compliance with relevant obligations under international human rights law, and that safety and security risks are prevented, addressed, and eliminated and to strengthen the capacity of women and girls to create, manage, control, and have ownership of their personal data.
2 Ensure users have the right to access their personal data and to obtain correction, deletion, and blocking of it.
3 Provide users with relevant information at all stages of processing, using clear and plain language.
4 Inform users clearly about the conditions under which they may exercise the right to personal data erasure, to object to the processing of data and to withdraw consent provided for the processing of personal data, following which all processing based on the consent of the user should be terminated.

[Staff]

1 Establish clear and specific standards on the working conditions (e.g. pay, training, performance quotas, working hours, the allocation of sufficient time for assessing content and opportunities to seek professional support and qualified legal advice where necessary) of all platform staff working on content moderation. These should also apply to staff working on behalf of a platform via outsourcing companies.
2 Limit exposure to traumatic content as much as possible and provide moderators with adequate support.
3 Build multi-disciplinary teams, including gender experts, representatives of the social sciences, and other domain experts.

[Reporting and transparency]

1 Publish annual transparency report on the number of reported illegal and harmful content of cyberviolence against women, the type and number of items of content reported and removed, together with a country breakdown and their proof of due diligence in responding to these types of violence, including descriptions of the departments and staff responsible for responding to content complaints, the support and training that staff members and content moderators receive to handle complaints, and description of the personnel and expertise responding to harassment complaints – in all relevant languages.
2 Allow external independent audits, conducted either by a dedicated agency or other independent bodies.
3 Allow trusted research institutions and civil society organizations (CSOs) to access anonymized and disaggregated data about content removals and complaints submitted to the platforms, including the type of action taken and the time it takes to review reported content.
4 Collect and publish gender and age disaggregated data in partnership with CSOs that provide insight into the scale and nature of cyberviolence against women and girls.

[Cooperation with law-enforcement agencies]

1 As first responders ensure that evidences of cyberviolence against women are retained for future effective criminal law investigations.
2 Report cyberviolence against women as illegal content to a law-enforcement agency.
3 Provide law-enforcement agency with all information needed upon request to ensure effective criminal law investigations.

[Cooperation with women's rights NGOs]

1 Co-operate with NGOs working on violence against women, domestic violence responders, and feminist cybersecurity experts, including local ones, to respond to cyberviolence in local contexts.
2 Consult NGOs to ensure that the complaint mechanisms, terms and conditions, and policies are designed, implemented, evaluated, and improved through participatory processes.
3 Provide financial support to NGOs working on cyberviolence against women and fund digital citizenship education initiatives.
4 Cooperate with NGOs, including anti-racist, LGBTQI+ and women's advocacy organizations, and with academics and researchers to fund research on gender-based cyberviolence.

5 Engage with external and independent mitigation efforts such as community advisory boards/panels and external audits.
6 Create a cross-platform consortium with a participation of women's rights NGOs and advocacies to track and respond to cyberviolence against women.

Annex

Laws and soft laws

Directive 2012/29/EU of the European Parliament and of the Council of 25 October 2012 establishing minimum standards on the rights, support, and protection of victims of crime and replacing Council Framework Decision 2001/220/JHA, https://eur-lex.europa.eu/legal-content/EN/TXT/HTML/?uri=CELEX%3A32012L0029

Group of Experts on Action against Violence against Women and Domestic Violence (GREVIO), 'GREVIO General Recommendation No. 1 on the digital dimension of violence against women', October 20, 2021, https://rm.coe.int/grevio-rec-no-on-digital-violence-against-women/1680a49147

Recommendation CM/Rec(2018)2 of the Committee of Ministers to Member States on the roles and responsibilities of internet intermediaries, https://rm.coe.int/1680790e14

Recommendation CM/Rec(2019)1 of the Committee of Ministers to member States on preventing and combating sexism, https://rm.coe.int/168093b26a

Regulation (EU) 2022/2065 of the European Parliament and of the Council of 19 October 2022 on a Single Market for Digital Services and amending Directive 2000/31/EC (Digital Services Act), https://eur-lex.europa.eu/legal-content/EN/TXT/?uri=CELEX%3A32022R2065

Reports, studies, and analysis of the bodies, institutions, and agencies of the United Nations, the Council of Europe, and the European Union

Artificial intelligence and gender equality. Key findings of UNESCO's Global Dialogue, 2020, https://unesdoc.unesco.org/ark:/48223/pf0000374174

Commission on the Status of Women, CSW67 Agreed Conclusions, 'Innovation and technological change, and education in the digital age for achieving gender equality and the empowerment of all women and girls', 67. Session, March 6–7, 2023, https://documents.un.org/doc/undoc/ltd/n23/081/71/pdf/n2308171.pdf

European Institute for Gender Equality, 'Combating Cyber Violence against Women and Girls', November 25, 2022, https://eige.europa.eu/publications resources/publications/combating-cyber-violence-against-women-and-girls

European Parliament, Policy Department for Citizens' Rights and Constitutional Affairs, 'Social media platforms and challenges for democracy, rule of law and fundamental rights', April 2023, www.europarl.europa.eu/RegData/etudes/STUD/2023/743400/IPOL_STU(2023)743400_EN.pdf

European Parliamentary Research Service, 'Combating gender-based violence: Cyber violence. European added value assessment', March 2021, www.europarl.europa.eu/RegData/etudes/STUD/2021/662621/EPRS_STU(2021)662621_EN.pdf

Organization of American States: Inter-American Committee against Terrorism (CICTE), Inter-American Commission of Women (CIM), 'Online gender-based violence against women and girls. Guide of basic concepts', 2021, www.oas.org/en/sms/cicte/docs/Guide-basic-concepts-Online-gender-based-violence-against-women-and-girls.pdf

A. van der Wilk, 'Protecting women and girls from violence in the digital age. The relevance of the Istanbul Convention and the Budapest Convention on Cybercrime in addressing online and technology-facilitated violence against women', Council of Europe, 2021, https://edoc.coe.int/en/violence-against-women/10686-protecting-women-and-girls-from-violence-in-the-digital-age.html

UNESCO, 'Your opinion doesn't matter, anyway. Exposing technology-facilitated gender-based violence in an era of generative AI', 2023, https://unesdoc.unesco.org/ark:/48223/pf0000387483

UNFPA, 'What is technology-facilitated gender-based violence?', 2023, www.unfpa.org/resources/brochure-what-technology-facilitated-gender-based-violence

United Nations, General Assembly, 'Intensification of efforts to eliminate all forms of violence against women and girls. Report of the Secretary General', August 18, 2022, https://documents.un.org/doc/undoc/gen/n22/465/68/pdf/n2246568.pdf

United Nations Human Rights, 'Report of the Special Rapporteur on violence against women, its causes and consequences on online violence against women and girls from a human rights perspective', June 18, 2018, https://documents.un.org/doc/undoc/gen/g18/184/58/pdf/g1818458.pdf

Reports, studies, and analysis of NGOs, CSOs, and experts

K. Baekgaard, 'Technology-facilitated gender-based violence. An emerging issue in women, peace and security', Georgetown Institute for Women, Peace and Security, 2024, https://giwps.georgetown.edu/wp-content/uploads/2024/06/Technology-Facilitated-Gender-Based-Violence.pdf

End Violence against Women Coalition and Glitch UK, 'The ripple effect. COVID-19 and the epidemic of online abuse', 2020, www.endviolenceagainstwomen.org.uk/online-abuse-during-covid-almost-half-of-women-have-experienced-online-abuse-during-pandemic/

European Women's Lobby, '#HerNetHerRights. Mapping the state of online violence against women and girls in Europe', 2017, www.womenlobby.org/IMG/pdf/hernetherrights_report_2017_for_web.pdf

Generation G partnership, 'Decoding technology-facilitated gender-based violence: a reality check from seven countries', 2024, https://rutgers.international/resources/decoding-technology-facilitated-gender-based-violence-a-reality-check-from-seven-countries/

GenPol – Gender & Policy Insights, 'When Technology Meets Misogyny. Multi-level, Intersectional Solutions to Digital Gender-Based Violence', 2020, www.thewomensorganisation.org.uk/wp-content/uploads/2020/09/When-Technology-Meets-Misogyny-GenPol-Policy-Paper-2.pdf

N. Jankowicz *et al.*, 'Malign creativity. How gender, sex, and lies are weaponized against women online', Wilson Center, January 2021, www.wilsoncenter.org/sites/default/files/media/uploads/documents/Report%20Malign%20Creativity%20How%20Gender%2C%20Sex%2C%20and%20Lies%20are%20Weaponized%20Against%20Women%20Online_0.pdf

Plan International, 'State of the World's Girls 2020: Free to Be Online. A report on girls' and young women's experiences of online harassment', 2020, https://plan-international.org/publications/free-to-be-online/

K. Standish, 'Technology-facilitated gender-based violence and democracy', TODA Peace Institute, 2023, https://toda.org/assets/files/resources/policy-briefs/t-pb-181_gender-based-violence-and-democracy_standish.pdf

Instead of a final conclusion

It may take 134 years to achieve full gender parity at the current rate of progress.[1] It would take even longer if we don't start to combat cyberviolence against women. There is no time to lose, there is no room for baby steps. We need to look at who benefits from this and who loses. We need to ask ourselves the question whether we are on the side of the victim or the side of the perpetrator.

Women experiencing cyberviolence often hear 'it's not a big deal'. Cyberviolence is usually minimized and normalized. It's wrong. Research on the scale and the extent of cyberviolence against women, its roots and consequences indicates 'it's a big deal'. Cyberviolence affects not only women's health, lives, and future, but the entire society. And it's getting worse since the technology develops. Existing laws are siloed and fragmented. Social media platforms are not held accountable.

Cyberviolence against women needs to be addresses in legislation to protect victims efficiently. The list of recommendations, collected for the first time from various reports and studies, attempts to establish a path to combat cyberviolence against women.

Note

1 World Economic Forum, 'Global Gender Gap Report', 2024, www.weforum.org/publications/global-gender-gap-report-2024/

DOI: 10.4324/9781003683193-5

Bibliography

Abdul Aziz Z., 'Due diligence and accountability for online violence against women', July 31, 2017, www.apc.org/en/pubs/due-diligence-and-accountability-online-violence-against-women

Amnesty International, 'Poland: "A Thousand Cuts" technology-facilitated gender-based violence against Poland's LGBTI community on X', September 1, 2025, www.amnesty.org/en/documents/eur37/0098/2025/en/

Amnesty International, '#ToxicTwitter. Violence and abuse against women online', 2018, www.amnestyusa.org/wp-content/uploads/2018/03/Toxic-Twitter.pdf

Association for Progressive Communications, 'End violence case studies', 2015, www.genderit.org/articles/protecting-right-freedom-expression-strategies-survivors-tech-related-violence-against

Baekgaard K., 'Technology-facilitated gender-based violence. An emerging issue in women, peace and security', *Georgetown Institute for Women, Peace and Security*, 2024, https://giwps.georgetown.edu/wp-content/uploads/2024/06/Technology-Facilitated-Gender-Based-Violence.pdf

Bailey J., Burkell J., Dunn S., Gosse Ch., Steeves V., 'AI and Technology-Facilitated Violence and Abuse', (in:) *Artificial Intelligence and the Law in Canada*, eds. F. Martin-Bariteau, T. Scassa, LexisNexis Canada, 2021.

Barker K., Jurasz O., '#MeToo, sport, and women: foul, own goal, or touchdown? Online abuse of women in sport as a contemporary issue', (in:) *Sports and Human Rights*, eds. V. Boillet, S. Weerts, A.R. Ziegler, Springer, 2024.

Barker K., Jurasz O., *Online Misogyny as Hate Crime: A Challenge for Legal Regulation?*, Routledge, 2019.

Barrett P.M., 'Some facts about fact-checking: defending the imperfect search for truth in an era of institutionalized lying', January 27, 2025, www.techpolicy.press/some-facts-about-fact-checking-defending-the-imperfect-search-for-truth-in-an-era-of-institutionalized-lying/

Brown A., 'Models of governance of online hate speech', *Council of Europe* 2020, https://edoc.coe.int/en/fundamental-freedoms/10357-models-of-governance-of-online-hate-speech.html

'Bumble and safety experts call for EU to ban cyberflashing and A.I. image abuse', https://bumble-buzz.com/bumble-cyberflashing-ai-eu-policy/

CEDAW Committee, 'General recommendation No. 35 (2017) on gender-based violence against women, updating general recommendation No. 19 (1992)', July 26, 2017, www.ohchr.org/en/documents/general-comments-and-recommendations/general-recommendation-no-35-2017-gender-based

Ciesiołkiewicz K., 'Środowisko cyfrowe – w pułapce przemocy instytucjonalnej' ('The Digital Environment – in the Trap of Institutional Violence'), (in:) *Internet dzieci. Raport z monitoringu obecności dzieci i młodzieży w internecie (Internet of Children. A Report on the Monitoring of the Presence of Children and Adolescents on the Internet)*, eds. M. Bigaj, K. Ciesiołkiewicz, K. Mikulski, A. Miotk, J. Przewłocka, M. Rosa, A. Załęska, Fundacja Instytut Cyfrowego Obywatelstwa (Institute for Digital Citizenship Foundation) oraz Państwowa Komisja do spraw przeciwdziałania wykorzystaniu seksualnemu małoletnich poniżej lat 15 (State Committee for Counteracting Sexual Abuse of Minors Below 15 Years of Age), 2025, https://cyfroweobywatelstwo.pl/internetdzieci/

Collins P.H., 'Intersectionality's definitional dilemmas', *Annual Review of Sociology* 2015/41(1), pp. 1–20, https://doi.org/10.1146/annurev-soc-073014-112142.

Commission on the Status of Women, CSW67 Agreed Conclusions, 'Innovation and technological change, and education in the digital age for achieving gender equality and the empowerment of all women and girls', 67. Session, March 6–7, 2023, https://documents.un.org/doc/undoc/ltd/n23/081/71/pdf/n2308171.pdf

Council of Europe, 'Cyberviolence. Germany: regulations for service providers', www.coe.int/en/web/cyberviolence/germany

Council of Europe, 'Encouraging the participation of the private sector and the media in the prevention of violence against women and domestic violence: article 17 of the Istanbul Convention. A collection of papers on the Council of Europe Convention on preventing and combating violence against women and domestic violence', January 2016, https://rm.coe.int/16805970bd

Council of Europe, 'Types of cyberviolence', www.coe.int/en/web/cyberviolence/types-of-cyberviolence

Council of Europe Commissioner for Human Rights, Dunja Mijatović, 'Safeguarding human rights in the era of artificial intelligence', July 3, 2018, www.coe.int/en/web/commissioner/-/safeguarding-human-rights-in-the-era-of-artificial-intelligence

Crenshaw K., 'Mapping the margins: intersectionality, identity politics, and violence against women of color', *Stanford Law Review* 1991/43(6), pp. 1241–1299, https://doi.org/10.2307/1229039.

Cyber Civil Rights Initiative, 'End revenge porn. A Campaign of the Cyber Civil Rights Initiative, Inc.', www.cybercivilrights.org/wp-content/uploads/2014/12/RPStatistics.pdf

Cybercrime Convention Committee (T-CY), Working Group on Cyberbullying and Other Forms of Online Violence, Especially against Women and Children, 'Mapping study on cyberviolence', July 9, 2018, https://rm.coe.int/t-cy-2017-10-cbg-study-provisional/16808c4914

Digital Rights Foundation, 'Policy paper. Perspectives on gender disinformation', 2021, https://digitalrightsfoundation.pk/work/research/

Duggan M., 'Online harassment', Pew Research Center, October 22, 2014, www.pewinternet.org/2014/10/22/online-harassment/

Duggan M., 'Online harassment', Pew Research Center, July 11, 2017, www.pewresearch.org/internet/2017/07/11/online-harassment-2017/

Dunn S., 'Technology-facilitated gender-based violence: an overview', December 7, 2020, www.cigionline.org/publications/technology-facilitated-gender-based-violence-overview/

End Violence against Women Coalition and Glitch UK, 'The ripple effect. COVID-19 and the epidemic of online abuse', 2020, https://glitchcharity.co.uk/covid19/

eSafety Commissioner of Australia, '"For my safety". Experiences of technology-facilitated abuse among women with intellectual disability or cognitive disability', August 2021, www.esafety.gov.au/sites/default/files/2021-09/TFA%20WWICD_accessible.pdf

European Institute for Gender Equality, 'Combating cyber violence against women and girls', November 25, 2022, https://eige.europa.eu/publications-resources/publications/combating-cyber-violence-against-women-and-girls

European Parliament, Policy Department for Citizens' Rights and Constitutional Affairs, 'Cyber violence and hate speech online against women', September 2018, www.europarl.europa.eu/RegData/etudes/STUD/2018/604979/IPOL_STU(2018)604979_EN.pdf

European Parliament's Policy Department for Citizens' Rights and Constitutional Affairs, 'The impact of the use of social media on women and girls', March 2023, www.europarl.europa.eu/RegData/etudes/STUD/2023/743341/IPOL_STU(2023)743341_EN.pdf

European Parliament's Policy Department for Citizens' Rights and Constitutional Affairs, 'The legislative frameworks for victims of gender-based violence (including children) in the 27 Member States', October 2022, www.europarl.europa.eu/RegData/etudes/STUD/2022/738126/IPOL_STU(2022)738126_EN.pdf

European Parliament, Policy Department for Citizens' Rights and Constitutional Affairs, 'Social media platforms and challenges for democracy, rule of law and fundamental rights', April 2023, www.europarl.europa.eu/RegData/etudes/STUD/2023/743400/IPOL_STU(2023)743400_EN.pdf

European Parliamentary Research Service, 'Combating gender-based violence: cyber violence. European added value assessment', March 2021, www.europarl.europa.eu/RegData/etudes/STUD/2021/662621/EPRS_STU(2021)662621_EN.pdf

European Parliamentary Research Service, 'Measures to address cyber-violence against women in EU Member States and Canada, UK, US', prepared at the request of MEP S. Spurek, 2024.

European Union Agency for Fundamental Rights, 'Challenges to women's human rights in the EU. Gender discrimination, sexist hate speech and gender-based violence against women and girls', November 2017, https://fra.europa.eu/sites/default/files/fra_uploads/fra-2017-challenges-to-women-human-rights_en.pdf

European Union Agency for Fundamental Rights, 'Violence against women: an EU-wide survey. Results at a glance', 2014, https://fra.europa.eu/sites/default/files/fra-2014-vaw-survey-at-a-glance-oct14_en.pdf

European Women's Lobby, '#HerNetHerRights. Mapping the state of online violence against women and girls in Europe', 2017, www.womenlobby.org/IMG/pdf/hernetherrights_report_2017_for_web.pdf

Flynn A., Henry N., 'Image-based sexual abuse: an Australian reflection', *Women & Criminal Justice* 2021/31(4), pp. 313–326, https://doi.org/10.1080/08974454.2019.1646190

Freedom House, 'Freedom on the net 2024, Germany', 2024, https://freedomhouse.org/country/germany/freedom-net/2024

Generation G partnership, 'Decoding technology-facilitated gender-based violence: a reality check from seven countries', 2024, https://rutgers.international/resources/decoding-technology-facilitated-gender-based-violence-a-reality-check-from-seven-countries/

GenPol – Gender & Policy Insights, 'When technology meets misogyny. Multi-level, intersectional solutions to digital gender-based violence', 2020, www.thewomensorganisation.org.uk/wp-content/uploads/2020/09/When-Technology-Meets-Misogyny-GenPol-Policy-Paper-2.pdf

Giugni L., *The Threat: Why Digital Capitalism is Sexist. And How to Resist*, September Publishing, 2022.

Group of Experts on Action against Violence against Women and Domestic Violence (GREVIO), 'GREVIO general recommendation No. 1 on the digital dimension of violence against women', October 20, 2021, https://rm.coe.int/grevio-rec-no-on-digital-violence-against-women/1680a49147

Group of Experts on Action against Violence against Women and Domestic Violence (GREVIO), 'Report submitted by Spain pursuant to Article 68, paragraph 1 of the Council of Europe Convention on preventing and combating violence against women and domestic violence (1st thematic evaluation round)', February 13, 2024, https://rm.coe.int/grevio-inf-2024-1-spain-1st-thematic-evaluation-round-eng/1680ae0c38

Hern A., 'Feminist games critic cancels talk after terror threat', October 15, 2014, www.theguardian.com/technology/2014/oct/15/anita-sarkeesian-feminist-games-critic-cancels-talk

Hinduja S., Patchin J.W., 'Cyberstalking laws', *Cyberbullying Research Center*, 2023, https://cyberbullying.org/cyberstalking-laws

Instytut Zamenhofa [Zamenhof Institute], 'Dezinformacja jako forma przemocy wobec kobiet w Polsce' ('Disinformation as a form of violence against women'), 2024, https://zamenhof.pl/2024/10/16/dezinformacja-jako-forma-przemocy-wobec-kobiet-w-polsce-przeczytaj-raport-instytutu-zamenhofa/

Inter-Parliamentary Union, 'Sexism, harassment and violence against women in parliaments in Africa', 2021, www.ipu.org/resources/publications/issue-briefs/2021-11/sexism-harassment-and-violence-against-women-in-parliaments-in-africa

Jankowicz N. et al., 'Malign creativity. How gender, sex, and lies are weaponized against women online', *Wilson Center*, January 2021, www.wilsoncenter.org/sites/default/files/media/uploads/documents/Report%20Malign%20Creativity%20How%20Gender%2C%20Sex%2C%20and%20Lies%20are%20Weaponized%20Against%20Women%20Online_0.pdf

Jurasz O., 'Online violence against women: a four nations study', The Open University, 2024, https://oro.open.ac.uk/96398/

Jurasz O., Barker K., 'Online text-based (sexual) abuse', (in:) *Gender-Based Violence. A Comprehensive Guide*, eds. P. Ali, M. Rogers, Springer, 2023, https://link.springer.com/chapter/10.1007/978-3-031-05640-6_38

Kaplan K.A., 'Facemash creator survives Ad board', *The Harvard Crimson*, November 19, 2003, www.thecrimson.com/article/2003/11/19/facemash-creator-survives-ad-board-the/

Kelly L., *Surviving Sexual Violence*, Polity Press, 1988.

Kirchengast T., Crofts T., 'The legal and policy contexts of 'revenge porn' criminalisation: the need for multiple approaches', *Oxford University Commonwealth Law Journal* 2019/19(1), pp. 1–29, https://doi.org/10.1080/14729342.2019.1580518

Krook M.L., 'Semiotic violence against women: theorizing harms against female politicians', *Journal of Women in Culture and Society* 2022/47(2), pp. 371–397, https://doi.org/10.1086/716642.

Krook M.L., Restrepo Sanín J., 'The cost of doing politics? Analyzing violence and harassment against female politicians', *Perspectives on Politics* 2020/18(3), pp. 740–755, https://doi.org/10.1017/S1537592719001397.

Lenhart A. et al., 'Online harassment, digital abuse, and cyberstalking in America', *Data & Society*, November 21, 2016, https://datasociety.net/library/online-harassment-digital-abuse-cyberstalking/

Lewis R., Rowe M., Wiper C., 'Online abuse of feminists as an emerging form of violence against women and girls', *The British Journal of Criminology* 2017/57(6), pp. 1462–1481, https://doi.org/10.1093/bjc/azw073.

McGlynn C. et al., 'It's Torture for the soul. The harms of image-based sexual abuse', *Social & Legal Studies* 2021/30(4), pp. 541–562, https://doi.org/10.1177/0964663920947791

McGlynn C., Woods L., Antoniou A., 'Pornography, the online safety act 2023 and the need for further reform', August 18, 2024, https://ssrn.com/abstract=4928796

Mishra V., 'General assembly adopts landmark resolution on artificial intelligence', March 21, 2024, https://news.un.org/en/story/2024/03/1147831

National Democratic Institute, '#NotTheCost. Stopping violence against women in politics. A call to action', 2016, www.ndi.org/sites/default/files/1%20%23NotTheCost%20-%20Call%20to%20Action.pdf

National Democratic Institute, 'Tweets that chill. Analyzing online violence against women in politics. Report of case study research in Indonesia, Colombia, and Kenya', 2019, www.ndi.org/sites/default/files/NDI%20Tweets%20That%20Chill%20Report.pdf

NORC at the University of Chicago and International Center for Research on Women, 'Landscape analysis of technology-facilitated gender-based violence. Findings from the Asia Region', February 2022, www.icrw.org/wp-content/uploads/2021/09/USAID-TFGBV-Landscape-Analysis-Asia.pdf

O'Brien S.R., Fernández N.P., '2022 Global Symposium on technology-facilitated gender based violence results. building a common pathway', *Wilson Center and UNFPA*, September 27, 2023, www.wilsoncenter.org/publication/2022-global-symposium-technology-facilitated-gender-based-violence-results-building

Opinion of European Economic and Social Committee, 'Combating violence against women', 2022, www.eesc.europa.eu/en/our-work/opinions-information-reports/opinions/combatting-violence-against-women

Organization for Security and Cooperation in Europe (OSCE), Representative on Freedom of the Media, 'New challenges to freedom of expression. Countering online abuse of female journalists', 2016, www.osce.org/files/f/documents/c/3/220411.pdf

Organization of American States: Inter-American Committee against Terrorism (CICTE), Inter-American Commission of Women (CIM), 'Online gender-based violence against women and girls. Guide of basic concepts', 2021, www.oas.org/en/sms/cicte/docs/Guide-basic-concepts-Online-gender-based-violence-against-women-and-girls.pdf

Plan International, 'State of the world's girls 2020: free to be online. A report on girls' and young women's experiences of online harassment', 2020, https://plan-international.org/publications/free-to-be-online/

Richardson-Self L., 'Hate speech against women online. Concepts and Countermeasures', *Lanham*, 2021.

Rigotti C., McGlynn C., 'Image-based sexual abuse and EU law: a critical analysis', *German Law Journal* 2024, pp. 1472–1493, www.cambridge.org/core/journals/german-law-journal/article/imagebased-sexual-abuse-and-eu-law-a-critical-analysis/B0CF334A0037DE3CA2067B79F506EB87

Rigotti C., McGlynn C., 'Towards an EU criminal law on violence against women: the ambitions and limitations of the commission's proposal to criminalise image-based sexual abuse', *New Journal of European Criminal Law* 2022/13(4), pp. 452–477, https://doi.org/10.1177/20322844221140713

Salazar L.R., Amores-Villalba A., Larrañaga E., Yubero S., Navarro R., 'Cyberbullying of university faculty: an examination of gender differences in cyberbullying victimization in higher education', *Computers in Human Behavior* 2024/155(C), pp. 108–186, https://doi.org/10.1016/j.chb.2024.108186.

Sękowska-Kozłowska K., Baranowska G., Gliszczyńska-Grabias A., 'Sexist hate speech and the international human rights law. Towards legal recognition of the phenomenon by the United Nations and the Council of Europe', *International Journal of the Semiotics of Law* 2022/35, pp. 2323–2345, https://doi.org/10.1007/s11196-022-09884-8

Shepherd T., 'More women turning off politics after Julia Gillard was badly treated', *The Advertiser*, January 14, 2014, www.adelaidenow.com.au/news/south-australia/more-women-turning-off-politics-after-julia-gillard-was-badly-treated/news-story/321177664cf100e0316704bad5c5f8a6

Sherry M., Olsen T., Vedele J.S., *Disability Hate Speech: Social, Cultural and Political Contexts*, Routledge, 2020.

Siapera E., 'Online misogyny as witch hunt: primitive accumulation in the age of techno-capitalism', (in:) *Gender Hate Online*, eds. D. Ging, E. Siapera, Palgrave Macmillan, 2019, https://doi.org/10.1007/978-3-319-96226-9_2

Silva de Alwis R. de, 'A Rapidly shifting landscape. Why digitized violence is the newest category of gender-based violence', *La Revue des Juristes de Sciences Po* 2024/25, p. 62, *U of Penn Law School, Public Law Research Paper* No. 23–43, https://ssrn.com/abstract=4648409

'Slovakian president Čaputová says she will not run for re-election', *The Guardian*, June 20, 2023, www.theguardian.com/world/2023/jun/20/slovakia-president-zuzana-caputova-says-she-will-not-run-for-re-election

Smahel D., Machackova H., Mascheroni G., Dedkova L., Staksrud E., Ólafsson K., Livingstone S., Hasebrink U., 'EU kids online 2020: survey results from 19 countries', *EU Kids Online, London School of Economics and Political Science*, 2020, https://eprints.lse.ac.uk/103294/

Sobieraj S., *Credible Threat: Attacks Against Women Online and the Future of Democracy*, Oxford University Press, 2020.

Spurek S., 'Analysis of the Victims' Rights Directive from a gender perspective', *European Institute for Gender Equality*, April 16, 2016, https://eige.europa.eu/publications-resources/publications/analysis-victims-rights-directive-gender-perspective?language_content_entity=en

Spurek S., 'Cyberprzemoc wobec kobiet w Polsce. Raport z badan' ('Cyberviolence against women in Poland. Survey report'), 2024, https://sylwiaspurek.pl/

Standish K., 'Technology-facilitated gender-based violence and democracy', *TODA Peace Institute*, 2023, https://toda.org/assets/files/resources/policy-briefs/t-pb-181_gender-based-violence-and-democracy_standish.pdf

The Economist Intelligence Unit, 'Measuring the prevalence of online violence against women', March 1, 2021, https://onlineviolencewomen.eiu.com/

UNESCO, 'Artificial intelligence and gender equality. Key findings of UNESCO's Global Dialogue', 2020, https://unesdoc.unesco.org/ark:/48223/pf0000374174

UNESCO, 'The Chilling. Global trends in online violence against women journalists', 2021, https://unesdoc.unesco.org/ark:/48223/pf0000377223

UNESCO, 'Your opinion doesn't matter, anyway. Exposing technology-facilitated gender-based violence in an era of generative AI', 2023, https://unesdoc.unesco.org/ark:/48223/pf0000387483

UNFPA, 'Technology-facilitated gender-based violence: making all spaces safe', December 1, 2021, www.unfpa.org/publications/technology-facilitated-gender-based-violence-making-all-spaces-safe

UNFPA, TFGBV Brochure, www.unfpa.org/sites/default/files/resource-pdf/TFGBV_Brochure-1000x560.pdf

United Nations Broadband Commission for Digital Development, Working Group on Broadband and Gender, 'Cyber violence against women and girls. A world-wide wake-up call', October 23, 2015, www.broadbandcommission.org/publication/cyber-violence-against-women/

United Nations, General Assembly, 'Intensification of efforts to eliminate all forms of violence against women and girls. Report of the secretary general', August 18, 2022, https://documents.un.org/doc/undoc/gen/n22/465/68/pdf/n2246568.pdf

United Nations Human Rights, 'A/76/258: Gender justice and freedom of expression – Report of the special rapporteur on the promotion and protection of the right to freedom of opinion and expression on gender justice and freedom of opinion and expression', July 30, 2021, www.ohchr.org/en/documents/thematic-reports/a76258-gender-justice-and-freedom-expression-report-special-rapporteur

United Nations Human Rights, 'The Impact of online violence on women human rights defenders and women's organisations', June 21, 2018, www.ohchr.org/en/statements/2018/06/impact-online-violence-women-human-rights-defenders-and-womens-organisations

United Nations Human Rights, 'Report of the special rapporteur on violence against women, its causes and consequences on online violence against women and girls from a human rights perspective', June 18, 2018, https://documents.un.org/doc/undoc/gen/g18/184/58/pdf/g1818458.pdf

UN Women, 'Accelerating efforts to tackle online and technology facilitated violence against women and girls (VAWG)', 2022, www.unwomen.org/sites/default/files/2022-10/Accelerating-efforts-to-tackle-online-and-technology-facilitated-violence-against-women-and-girls-en_0.pdf

UN-Women, Arab States, 'Violence against women in the online space: insights from a multi-country study in the Arab States', 2021, https://arabstates.unwomen.org/en/digital-library/publications/2021/11/violence-against-women-in-the-online-space

Valenti J., 'Anita Sarkeesian interview: "The word 'troll' feels too childish. This is abuse"', August 29, 2015, www.theguardian.com/technology/2015/aug/29/anita-sarkeesian-gamergate-interview-jessica-valenti van der Wilk A., 'Protecting women and girls from violence in the digital age. The relevance of the Istanbul convention and the budapest convention on cybercrime in addressing online and technology-facilitated violence against women', *Council of Europe*, 2021, https://edoc.coe.int/en/violence-against-women/10686-protecting-women-and-girls-from-violence-in-the-digital-age.html

Vogels E.A., 'The state of online harassment', Pew Research Center, January 13, 2021, www.pewresearch.org/wp-content/uploads/sites/20/2021/01/PI_2021.01.13_Online-Harassment_FINAL-1.pdf

Watson S., 'Online abuse of women: an interdisciplinary scoping review of the literature', *Feminist Media Studies* 2024/24(1), pp. 1–19, https://doi.org/10.1080/14680777.2023.2181136.

Whitaker A., 'Police investigating horrific catalogue of threats and abuse against Nicola Sturgeon', March 11, 2017, www.heraldscotland.com/news/15150383.police-investigating-horrific-catalogue-threats-abuse-nicola-sturgeon/

World Wide Web Foundation, 'Online gender-based violence and abuse: consultation briefing', 2021, https://uploads-ssl.webflow.com/61557f76c8a63ae527a819e6/615585a9bbfeb8836d512947_OGBV_ConsultationBriefing.pdf

Index